SUCCESS HANGOVER

SUCCESS HANGOVER

Ignite your next act.
Screw your status quo.
Feel alive again.

KELSEY RAMSDEN

LIONCREST
PUBLISHING

SUCCESS HANGOVER

Ignite your next act. Screw your status quo. Feel alive again.

ISBN   978-1-5445-1235-8 *Hardcover*

978-1-5445-1234-1 *Paperback*

978-1-5445-1233-4 *Ebook*

This one's for Andrew, Sophie, Graeme, and Sam.

Without you, there would be no me.

ACKNOWLEDGMENTS

I've found that my life and gratitude for those who have been a part of it have evolved over time, for reasons often I don't see until the evolution or lesson has settled in. So I'm reserving my thanks to you in this moment. Your thanks will come in time, and very much in person.

For now, I acknowledge the journey—

—oh, how I love you.

A VERY PERSONAL NOTE FOR THE CREATORS

No one made me do it—write this book. I wanted them to, but alas, it was I who had to pull this thing through my eye sockets and palm-sweating crisis of confidence to lay it before you...that you might sacrifice or understand it the way only we can.

Keep creating.

We are always ahead of them, and they can't understand or see it until we create it, and even then, sometimes not. But we do...those like us...so keep going.

The joy = the challenge.

An adapted Scottish blessing said often within my family

sums up the tension between exceptional and common, the experience of being a member of the minority like us.

Here's tay us; wha's like us. Damn few and the fewer the better.

CONTENTS

NOTES AND EXERCISES

HOW TO READ THIS BOOK

As with all work I do, I create things that provide a deep, intimate connection. This book is no different. It starts at the beginning and ends in the end.

In between, there are three sections:

- Admit It.
- Address It.
- Adapt to It.

Then, there is a bonus chapter.

Read this book how you like; do the exercises or don't. Get from it what you want.

My goal is to share some stories, hold up some mirrors, light some shadowy places, and in the end, provide you with brand-spankin'-new perspectives so you can develop a custom guide for you, by you.

I hope this book does for you what it did for me. It allowed me to see myself clearer, ignite my next act, screw my status quo, and feel alive again. I hope it does this so much for you that you share it with others like us, the people who are ready for what's next.

AN INVITATION

This book is just the beginning.

In concert with this book, I created a website at www. SuccessHangover.com to serve you and every reader like you in diving deep into the body of work.

I hope that you will take this invitation to visit the site for:

- Additional resources
- How-tos
- Exercises not included in this book
- Case studies
- Downloads
- Conversation guides
- Idea packets

You will also find my collection of the most recent and

relevant conversations on the subject, along with podcasts, recommendations for next steps, and connection to our community.

If you want to join me and other readers in our community, or simply come and take what you find in this book even further, then head on over to www.SuccessHangover.com.

I'll see you there.

Book One

———

ADMIT IT

INTRODUCTION

On January 14, 2001, revered French chef Alain Passard announced the unthinkable. He would take his three-star, Michelin-rated restaurant, Arpège, in a new direction by shifting away from meat-focused dishes to vegetable-based cuisine. Why, at the height of success and with three Michelin stars to gamble (the Holy Grail, only around sixty chefs have ever received), would he do such a thing—and in a meat-loving nation?

Passard's news rocked the culinary world. The haters took to their soapboxes, saying, "He'll fail. He's crazy. He'll lose his stars." The *New York Times* ran an article titled, "May the Force Be with Alain Passard." In other words, no one thought he'd pull it off. One could almost imagine *The Thinker* statue shaking his head from its bronze perch in the Rodin Museum gardens just steps outside the restaurant. Even Michelin declared the move courageous, and Passard admitted to the *New York Times*, "I am putting all the cards on the table. Putting myself and my entire career in question: my three stars, the public, my clients."

Guess what? The move paid off. Passard's vegetable dishes were interesting, provocative, and delicious. He kept his three stars, received global attention, earned his own episode on Netflix's *Chef's Table: France* series, and Arpège was named the nineteenth best restaurant in the world by S. Pellegrino World's 50 Best Restaurants. Passard knew he was taking a major risk, so why did he do it? Why change if you're doing OK, or in Passard's case, extremely well? History answers that question. What goes up must come down, unless—what?

We adapt.

Passard internally felt the need to adapt his menu. Yet to remain relevant, the world required him to change, too, even if it wasn't yet obvious to everyone else. No one tapped him on the shoulder and said, "Psst. Hey, big shot, you better mix things up before they get stale!" There was no tap, because life doesn't work that way. Passard defined what it is to be ahead of the curve. He futureproofed himself and became exceptional. He knew that success, if sat upon, diminishes. He took action to survive.

Chances are, if you're reading this book, it's because you're feeling restless. Maybe it's an itch now, a recurring inner voice. Or maybe you're at the other end of the spectrum and have already reached that "Dammit, I'm done with this!" phase. Whether you're at the top and living off your past accomplishments or stuck in the status quo, there's an underlying question—what's next?

Gravity pulls us toward obsolescence unless we stop and *defy it*.

WHAT'S STOPPING US?

We have good lives. They may not be great, but they're *good*. They're safe, comfortable. But humans were designed to evolve, and therefore, we can't help but wonder, is this it? After entertaining this question, we tell ourselves to simmer down. We think that if we change, people will say we're insane. Because things aren't terrible. They're—good. But at some point, good stops being good. It becomes mediocre. And like a virus, mediocrity spreads. Sales decrease, our relationships fizzle, we look for scapegoats. There's a cadence to success that inevitably slows until suddenly we wake up and think, "Wait a minute, I'm stuck. Stuck in the missionary sex of my career. It's decent, it counts, but it's hardly memorable."

STUCK IN THE MISSIONARY SEX OF
MY CAREER. IT'S DECENT, IT COUNTS
BUT IT'S HARDLY MEMORABLE.
                                    -KR

YourNextAct

WE ARE QUICKLY BECOMING OUTDATED

As you're reading this, the world is preparing to replace you. Most of what can be taught can be programmed. What can be programmed can become a robot's job.

It once was that you could guarantee someone success so long as he became a doctor or lawyer. Today, those professions are at the top of the line for artificial intelligence (AI) replacement. Our kids will have jobs that don't exist yet, so it's crazy to think we can plan our future selves with an outdated checklist. The tools we've always used for the future have stopped working.

VANILLA CAKE

Let's say you make the best vanilla cake in town—so, naturally, your sales are great. You've specialized in what you do, and to maintain your position, you keep stocking your shelves with the best ingredients for making vanilla cake. Everyone comes to you when they want it, and ultimately, you're at the top of your game. Then one day, the world changes, and little by little people are talking about blueberry streusel; before long, the whole market shifts, and it's blueberry streusel they want! Or maybe, like Alain Passard, *you* change and you're sick of vanilla cake. The problem? You've stocked your shelves with everything needed to make amazing vanilla cake—and that's it. You pigeonholed yourself and your career. Now what? You've got to go out and get some new ingredients.

We tend to listen to the same radio station, watch the same TV channel, read the same authors, go the same way to work, and drink the same coffee—because it's comfortable. We know what we like, and we stick with it because it's safe. Adaptation, however, requires exposure to something that's potentially unknown, unsafe, and even unpractical today. What, no results today? Why bother? So we keep on keeping on until we're bored as fuck—and we're no longer all that interesting either.

To survive one's own success, one must engage in futureproofing. The notion of futureproofing is to break free from the rut: screw stagnation, come alive again, and start act two by collecting ingredients (i.e., experiences, tools, knowledge, and people) to stock your shelves. The 3E Method encompasses the strategy to stocking the right ingredients so you're ready for anything, more satisfied—and a hell of a lot more intriguing to others and yourself.

How long ago was it when you took on an activity just for the sake of it? Most of what we do has an expectation for a direct resultant outcome. We do X because it does Y. We engage in predictable activities despite knowing innovation, creativity, and adaptation don't work that way. An innovation doesn't come with instructions; otherwise, it's already been done, hasn't it? You want and need to avoid becoming obsolete, both personally and professionally, which means the pressure's on now to come up with the next best thing.

How will you do it?

IT'S ABOUT THAT FEELING

When was your last breakthrough moment? One of those *fuck-yeah* flashes when your body tingles with excitement because you just figured something out and you know it. It might have been a brilliant idea, a solution, or even just a sexy hypothesis. Now answer this: where were you when it happened?

Albert Einstein did not come up with the theory of relativity sitting at his desk. Chances are, yours didn't happen at your desk either. Nor did it happen when you were doing the laundry, or driving your kids to school, or taking the train. You can't make ice cream in the sun. Why are we asking ourselves to do this?

Naturally, when we create false hope, we're going to be continually disappointed—and so ensues the downward spiral. Eventually, we undermine ourselves and enter a mundane, low-grade state of life. It becomes our new standard. It might look great on the outside, but on the inside, it's killing us.

The traditional education system teaches us to jump hoops, check boxes, listen, and regurgitate. It's like playing tennis. You hit to me; I hit back. There's no reason to do anything outside of that, because you weren't asked to, nor are you provided extra credit or a higher grade. In fact, you might be punished. I happen to be one of those people who was punished for not hitting the ball back the way I was taught, but we'll cover that in the next chapter. We do as we're told for the simple reason that mammals respond to positive feedback. Conversely, we repel whenever we receive negative feedback. We're taught to conform to a very specific performance, and it's that rigidity that ultimately stalls both our careers and our lives.

HOOP-JUMPING MONKEYS

As we progress in our careers, there are fewer hoops and even fewer cues. Just like there was no one to tap Chef Alain Passard on the shoulder and tell him to push his restaurant to a new level, people stop nudging us and reminding us to innovate, or even do something as simple as ask for a raise. Relationships suffer because our spouse stops reminding us to take him or her out on a date. Before long, we've stopped engaging in the world and with ourselves. We go to work, take the train, raise kids, and the space once used to innovate gets crowded out with all the things we think we *should* do.

Don't "should" on yourself.

To be fair, sometimes the signs are not that obvious. They're like cancer; internally your cells could be splitting, but you just don't know it yet—there are no visible symptoms. There's a hidden system, however: it's in your routine. Are you talking about the same thing frequently? Going to the same places? That's a symptom. Despite that the trigger points aren't always glaring, if you take a good hard moment to tune in with yourself, then honestly, you will know. You *do* know.

Alas, if you want to spur innovation, you need to get away from your desk. And by desk, I'm also talking about your safe and predictable little microcosm—everything from your routine coffee shop, to the way you get to work. You need to live off the page, or you'll be a caricature of yourself. Becoming exceptional requires you to adapt your life's tried-and-true recipes by slowly incorporating fresh, new ingredients. You must step out of your comfort zone, be open-minded and nimble—that's the baseline for an exceptional life, and one you feel alive within.

THE FUTUREPROOF APPROACH: THE ROAD TO EXCEPTIONALISM

What's your default future? If you continue on the path you're currently on without making any adaptations, where will you go? What does that future look like? If you can answer that in a way that makes you feel fabulous because you know you're on the path to greatness, then close this book. Give it to the person sitting beside you. If your default future is anything other than that, then as with most vices, you first need to **admit it**. After you've admitted it, you must **address it**. That leads us to the good stuff: **adaptation**. The good news? We'll start small. I'll explain how small, daily adaptations will light the way, no matter where you are headed.

But first, let's get down to business and work on the *admit it* part of your default future. Feels scary and too soon, right? Sorry, not sorry...because you're ready. That's why you're reading this book. Deep down, you know it's time.

Head to the back of the book and complete the Default Future Exercise. If you can't imagine defacing a book, I've got you covered—simply visit www.SuccessHangover. com and print it off for your writing pleasure.

When you ask yourself what you want your future to look like, resist the temptation to think about all the things you want to do. This isn't a book about bucket lists. Try inverting the question. What's *not* your future? It could be your career. It could be your relationship. It could be the way you're feeling.

I pause to note that this book is full of exercises that are meant to enrich your reading experience, among other things. They are somewhat front-loaded, so don't get overwhelmed and have the exercises drag you down if you showed up for a breezy read. However, if you showed up to dive deep, hit up the full exercise titled What I Do Not Want to complete this exercise before being propelled forward.

The futureproof approach puts you on course to become more competitive, successful, fascinating, and most importantly, alive. The more fascinating part refers to your personal world, your level of curiosity, and your ability to attract other people, including your own interest. The successful terms refer to your career and applicability. Throughout this book, I'll share my experiences first of what I did myself, and then how I coach business leaders to become more innovative and instigate more aha moments, ignite act two in your life, and as a by-product, you'll be the most interesting and relevant person in the room (between your ears, too). We will talk about how the 3E Method means better performance at work and at home, but more than that, it's about feeling more alive and connected to your life—instantly reengaging with yourself.

We're talking about being exceptional, not just better.

FANTASIES VS DREAMS

Before pulling our hypothetical Porsche into the fast lane, let's pump the brakes and gut-check everything. There's a difference between a fantasy and a dream, just like there's a difference between lust and love. Lust is short term. Lust is good only in the good times. It's hooking up with that hot guy or girl only to have him or her ruin it by saying something oppressive. Poof. Spell broken. Lust doesn't endure, and ever so conveniently, when one spell breaks, we just lust for something else.

It's natural to fantasize about alternate realities with our careers or relationships. When it's a fantasy, we'll use it when it's convenient. But if it's a dream, we'll never be fulfilled without it, and we'll chase it to the end. Simply put, a dream endures the inconvenient the way love does. We'll keep coming back to the gut-check because our fantasies are damn good at disguising themselves as dreams.

We need to take a good hard look at our dreams, too. Are you in a place of power but dreaming of chilling on the beach and writing books? Great. Will it afford you the life you currently have? Are you OK with it if it doesn't? Sometimes it's nicer to have a dream because life is hard. When an artist presents a magnificent piece of work, it was probably one of the hardest he's ever finished. It was torture. It's easy to assume Michelangelo woke up and sculpted David like it was a breeze. We overlook his tortured procedure and assume he had a divine, God-given talent. In this way, we give ourselves an excuse for having not reached his level.

FUTUREPROOFING IS ABOUT TAKING ACTION

You will finish this book with a plan. We'll work through a sliding scale of exercises from beginner to expert. You'll start by observing your life, becoming aware of your habits, traits, and behavior. Then you'll make daily adaptations that are unique to your goals. Futureproofing is an ongoing process that requires you to be constantly engaged.

Most of us know deep down if we've reached the summit and are happy to stop. What about you? Are you done, or is there more you want out of this one lovely dance on the blue planet?

Chapter 1

A SUCCESSFUL FAILURE

I started hustling when I was seven years old. The first person I got into business with? My four-year-old brother, Trent. We would barricade the end of our cul-de-sac and sweep the street during the day. Later, as the sun set over the Okanagan Mountains, a blaze of peach in the sky, the crickets beginning to chorus, our neighbors would make their way home, ready to chill with a Labatt and the Toronto Blue Jays baseball game. Except who did they see standing in their way? Trent and me—there to collect payment for our hard work and for allowing them to drive the newly cleaned street. Forget those been-done-before lemonade stands. We took neighborhood business to a new level. As the first family in the area to get a VCR, I recognized another opportunity. That big black rectangle was hardly plugged in before Trent and I were selling tickets to watch movies at our house. Need a mixtape? Sign one out, just ten cents a day with interest.

I remember thinking, "Hey, I'm pretty good. Something is going to happen." Of course, at that time, I thought maybe I was magical. But like many untarnished young minds, I was sure I'd excel at something—I just didn't know what yet. So I paid attention with every pursuit. Is this my thing? Luckily, my mom and dad afforded a lot of opportunities for me to try different activities and were equally pleased when I was OK at one as when I was great at another. When school started, however, it quickly told me all the things that were *not* my thing, which was pretty much everything academic. I remember feeling elated when I won an art prize in grade three, because I loved art. But it took only seconds for someone to bring me back down to earth: "Yeah, but you can't grow up to be an artist, Kelsey." So I scratched that idea.

I was the C kid. Teachers said I was so-so at math, and I believed it. Turns out I'm exceptional at math but didn't learn that until much later. I understood physics and solved all the problems. But I never earned full marks because I didn't solve them the way I'd been taught. I could write an amazing piece of poetry, but my grammar and my spelling were terrible—and again, I never excelled. The central thesis? I am not smart. That's what I was told, and I believed it. Yet I still had this nagging, an inner voice reminding me that I could figure stuff out.

Outside of academia, I was a social centerpiece: planning

parties, the captain of sports teams, and class clown, too. Not because I was the best; I wasn't the fastest or the prettiest, but I was friends with everyone. You know the best friend character to the leading role in the movie, the slightly chubby girl with glasses? That was me.

Following both society and my family's expectations, I went to university. Besides, that's where all the best parties were. I'd barely scraped through high school, and at college, I had to focus on getting enough credits to gain entrance to a university. When I finally accomplished that, I lived on and off academic probation. I recognized the university as a system of hoop jumping. I would cram for tests, regurgitate, and fully apply myself to earn As when I had to. After I'd built myself enough cushion to stay above water, I went back to slacking. Why bother losing so many hours studying for something you can look up in a book? No one was ever going to hold me at gunpoint on the street and ask for the cosine of an angle. And I wasn't going to be a surgeon, so why bother? When my friends would say, "Kelsey, you're not even going to show up for the Spanish final?" I wouldn't give it another thought. No. I was already failing Spanish. Why sit there two more hours just to confirm the thing I already knew: I would fail. Later, as they headed to the final, I'd wonder what was wrong with me. Why didn't I buy into the system?

After multiple failed attempts to convince anyone to

pose as me (for a cool $1,500) in the Calculus 100 exam, I predictably failed it. As a result, I had to switch my major from biology to economics, which led to a very difficult conversation with my parents. To switch from sciences to general arts was considered a downward move. But I found a niche in economics; the combination of math and business intrigued me. I saved my last ten units for easy classes such as guitar and art so I would finish strong. I knew the last ten credits were crucial when applying for a master's program, and there was still an internal voice telling me that I may be good enough to go on.

Then came the day. The fancy robe, the big stage, the bright lights, and endless applause. I got my diploma. I didn't jump up and down or festively toss my hat in the air. Instead, I remember thinking, "Really? That's it? All that strife and emotional turmoil, years of feeling like I wasn't good enough, and all I got was this piece of paper?" It was like five years of foreplay and no orgasm.

But fine. I'd checked the boxes and headed out into the big bad world with my piece of paper. Only problem was, the world didn't get my memo. The world kept on doing the same thing it always does—present more mildly intriguing hoops. That was the first crowning moment. I felt like I was being used. Is this all life is, a series of hoops to jump? If so, I knew one thing: my soul would die. And there's only one direction for our careers and personal relationships to go when that happens.

ROGER THAT, I'M IN THE MEDIOCRE ZONE, OVER

My first real job was on the side of the Alaska Highway. I was the fifteen-year-old flag girl slowing traffic and living in a trailer. There were forty men and one other woman (she was the cook and to my teenage mind, fell somewhere between forty and seventy years old). If being the only young person and girl wasn't enough to get me judged, I was also the boss's kid. The only way to save myself was to outwork everyone.

While my friends were partying over the summer, I'd call them on my two-way radio and struggle to hear them over the fuzz. "Yeah, roger that...you're going where? I can't hear you, over." Yes, it was depressing, but by the end of summer, I'd stashed as much as fifteen grand, which in the nineties and for a fifteen-year-old was a sweet lump of cash. After I graduated, I figured I could work in a coffee shop during the off-season and continue construction in the summer. But was this all I had to offer?

TURNING POINT: TAKE THIS EXIT

I remember sitting in the car with a dear friend, a hippie doctor. I was living in Victoria at the time, and we were driving to the ferry. As we were about to cross the blue waters, she turned to me and said, "Kelsey, if there's something you need to change, change it." My first reaction was defensive, and mentally I responded, *Is this some kind of 'prophecy-Burning-Man-I'm-more-in-tune-with-myself' comment?* Sensing my silent rebuff, she repeated what she'd said in its simplicity. If there's something to change, change it. That was the knife-twisting-into-my-heart moment. She saw it before I did, or maybe I wasn't willing to admit it to myself. What she said also sounded scary because the word *change* is scary.

It was the first time the world had me on the success track, and I was looking for my exit.

Here's the secret. We don't need to change; we only need to adapt. Futureproofing is about making daily adaptations, not metamorphosing into a totally new species. Of course, I didn't know that at the time, and I took her advice seriously. I made a big change, dumped the lovely fellow I had been living with for two years and left on a trip to India—alone. When I returned to Canada, however, it wasn't long before I fell back into the same rut. Same rut, different city, this time in Vancouver, where my brother lived. Trent and I were doing what many people in their tumultuous twenties on the West Coast were doing (fifteen years later, that same brother is turning heads and disrupting the medicinal marijuana industry as the founder of a publicly traded marijuana and life-style company, his second home-run business after being the founder of SAXX) and lost in a purple cloud when he said, "Hey, man, you gotta admit, we're in a mediocre zone right now." I thought about it and admitted he was right. Then I told him I'd always wanted to do my MBA to prove to Dad that I had some brains. The truth was, I fantasized about doing my PhD just to one-up him, because that's how damn competitive I am. My brother was all in as he already planned for the same long-term plan. So we addressed our state head-on: "OK, let's write our entrance exams."

The next day, we enrolled in a Kaplan class, the prep course for the GMAT. We studied and took it seriously. Time to wait and see what I scored.

THE FLUKE—OR WAS IT?

When I got my test score back, I was both elated and tremendously disappointed. Elated because I got a 580, which was basically the blind date of test scores—it meant I was in the game to apply, but odds that the other party would like me were really damn slim. It felt like proof once again I wasn't really that smart.

A couple of days later, a friend invited me for coffee. She brought along a mutual friend who had just been accepted to Western. Here I was, post-exams, asking, "What's Western?" only to learn the Richard Ivey School of Business at the University of Western Ontario was the best MBA school in Canada. I sipped my coffee thinking I should probably do some research. I assumed I'd never get into Western, but she'd planted the seed nevertheless.

I shelled out $250 per application and applied to all thirteen MBA schools in Canada. Soon, I ran to the mailbox each day awaiting my fate. It didn't take long for the skinny envelopes to come in the mail; the first rejection from none other than the worst MBA school in Canada. Thanks for your time and money. An ominous sign, yet I'm a gambler. I wasn't ready to say it was over. Skinny envelope after skinny envelope came—thanks, but no thanks. Then, finally a ray of hope from the University of British Columbia where my dad did his MBA. They requested an interview and told me they really liked my essay. I'd been tasked to come up with a unique storyline for television, and I proposed a reality TV show—this in the era before reality TV shows. A live call-in center would accept calls from the public and give direction to our "star." He was an ordinary Joe, except for the fact he's wearing an earpiece and instructed to do as he was told. If the callers said he should break up with his girlfriend, he had to do it. It was an experiment to see how society would handle him.

In the end, I didn't get accepted to UBC. By this point,

I'd been rejected twelve times, and only one envelope remained: Western. The best MBA school in Canada. It was a foregone conclusion, no point checking the mail. Then in August, just weeks before school would start, a big fat envelope from Western arrived—so fat I knew they had made a mistake. "Oh my God," I said to myself. "I better wire transfer the money like now." I ripped it open and found the cost: $100,000. I'd saved 70 percent of that from my summer construction work in case such a miracle would come my way. As for the rest, I had to call my dad. "You need how much?" he asked. "Wait, what did you do?"

The latter question goes to show where he thought I was heading in life. Naturally, he was thrilled to learn the real reason, and we wired the money that same day.

THE HEIST

I drove across the country in a two-seat convertible with a best friend, and upon arrival, I slept on a friend's couch before I finally felt confident enough to rent an apartment. I kept waiting for a punk scene to play out, expected hordes of people to shuffle out and laugh at me, tell me I didn't belong there. Finally, on the first day of class, I saw a name tag for me, a pile of books, my name on the class list, and I knew I was really in—I fooled them all.

I always wanted to be an art thief, and this was my heist. I could give up the dream of stealing art because I'd made off with a seat at the best MBA school in Canada, which was worth more in total lifetime earning potential than any piece of art I would have the guts to try and lift. All thieves fear they're about to get caught, and at school, I did, too. Every day I felt like an imposter. But I tried to fit in. I bought a new set of clothes—business suits, of course. I said adieu to my flip-flops and loose shirts. The only giveaway was Snot Rocket, my electric green Honda Civic del Sol, crystals jangling from the rearview mirror and shooting prisms wherever I went. It didn't matter how businessy I looked, anyone seeing me get out of that thing knew I was a hippie. Screw it. Snot Rocket was the first car in the lot in the morning and the last one out.

But six months into school, I got a reality check.

THE TRUTH COMES OUT

By nature—and yes, to maintain my heist—I was hyper-involved at Western, the chair of every committee, and I sat on the senate. What I loved most about school was engaging with and meeting new people. I started an initiative with a friend to help the university vet applicants. My aim was to expand their reach to accept applications from people like me, those who didn't have the best grades but had the people skills needed to run a business. Through it, I met Joanne, the woman in charge of admissions. She shook her head when she heard my name, a twinkle in her eye. "I remember your application," she said.

This was the moment. She was going to admit the mistake—that I wasn't supposed to be here.

"Did you know how you got in—onto the wait list at least?" No, I hadn't known. "Yes, I walked into the admissions room," she went on, "and saw your application on the top of the 'no' pile. It had a hand-drawn picture on the cover, so I just had to pick it up and read it. It struck me immediately. You'd answered a question on how you'd contribute something interesting to the school by drawing a picture, and you know what? I gave it to the admissions committee and said, 'Let this girl in. She's going to do something interesting.'"

The box-checking admissions committee had deemed me a "no." They wanted the safe lot, those with high test scores and a shit ton of community service hours. What had they thought when they'd seen my application? Whatever they thought, what matters is, I didn't compromise who I was in an attempt to get in, and it's not like my GMAT score could lie for me. I didn't tell them what they wanted to hear: *I'm a bright student. I'm dedicated. I have endless volunteer hours. I love puppies and walking grandmothers across the street!* It's what differentiated me from every other person with straight As, a 720 GMAT, and 800 volunteer hours. It may have been insane to send a hand-drawn picture to Canada's best MBA school, but my application got picked out of the pile because of it.

BYE-BYE BUSINESS SUITS

My first reaction to the fact that I'd come off the waiting list made me feel unwelcome. Then I turned it around and reconsidered. Maybe I belonged here more than a lot of the other people because I dared to do something different. The realization was like a precipitate chemistry experiment, the solutions mixing and swirling in a cloudy haze until suddenly they took form and shape. I had a new sense of clarity. I stopped wearing suits. I re-embraced my flip-flops, and I showed up being me. That's not to say I got straight As, but I went about doing my MBA the way I knew how to do it.

You can train a monkey to jump hoops, but you can't teach experience. The more vast and unique one's experiences, the harder he or she is to replicate. While so many race for the safe center, I stuck to the edges—wake-surfing where fewer boxes get checked.

Nothing against the center or the box-checkers, or the A+ earners—heaven knows I wished I had got more, but simply box-checking and straight A-earning is not where it's at today. It is the fastest way to a solid spot on the mediocre team.

I validated my lifestyle that day. And here's what it is: try something, do something, cling to the edge, get uncomfortable. Allow yourself to not make sense. Robots will take care of the things that can be taught. Renegades, the rest.

I'll stick with those renegades defying the principles that rely on the known and proven—the way it always has been. Because box-checking statistically significant predictors of success does not work, unless you're willing to be a statistic, proof of the mean or median.

Granted, some luck was involved in my admission—occasional flukes occur. Because that's life—and life is unpredictable. Yes, I had been originally rejected from Western, and if Joanne hadn't walked in at that moment, and if my application hadn't been on the top of the "no" pile, and if the drawing hadn't been face-up, a different fate may have played out. That's the luck part and it's what we don't control. But because I dared to be myself and do something different, my application jumped out and demanded attention. What were my odds with poor scores if I'd stuck to the predictable?

By the end of the second year, I was nominated for vale-

ROBOTS WILL TAKE CARE OF THE
THINGS THAT CAN BE TAUGHT.
RENEGADES, THE REST.
— KR

Your Next Act

dictorian, snubbing out a nomination for the guy on a full ride and with the second-highest GMAT in the whole class (who would later become my husband). I didn't win, but I was nominated in the top few. That was certainly enough to make me proud, but it got better. On graduation day, I learned that I'd won the MBAA Outstanding Contribution Award. And it's this honor out of all my certificates, diplomas, and awards that means the most. It meant that everyone I worked with at the MBA school decided that I had made the greatest impact on them and the program. Everybody can get an MBA if they jump through the right hoops. Not everybody can be the valedictorian, and not everybody can make a big enough splash to win such an award. It taught me that leadership is about sticking your neck out the way I did at school. Leadership is about speaking up, getting people on your side. Leadership is about defining what's next and showing people the way to join you—and having somewhere to lead them. But first, you *have to* lead yourself.

Thank you, Joanne, for reading my essay. Getting my MBA made an enormous difference, but the experiences while there, and those before and since, are what made me a success—and they will continue to. I used to be ashamed to admit I was let into MBA school as an outlier, but I could not be prouder today. I'm a renegade: adaptable and experienced—living out here where fewer boxes get checked, but success surely has happened.

Record scratch time. Despite my realizations and even the award, I did the expected after graduation. Like most MBA graduates, I became a consultant. What was I thinking? Apparently, I'd stopped thinking, because there I hovered in status quo for six months before I admitted to myself this path wasn't for me. I addressed my feelings, looked at my boss, and thought: If I had one hundred bucks to bet on her or me, who would I put in on?

I knew that I was the better bet, so I quit.

Now what? Better question: what did I love to do? Construction. I loved my old construction work. That was it. I was twenty-eight years old when my husband (the smarty-pants-now-consultant, what else?) and I moved back west, and I started my own construction company.

There I was, back to working twelve- to sixteen-hour days all over the province. Oh so glamorously, I lived on the side of the highway in a trailer. In the old days, I would go for beer with the crew after work. But now that I was the boss, it wasn't cool anymore. Instead, I spent my evening hours reading about how our brains are wired. Was there something different about my brain that made me a good leader? How was I able to accomplish a goal, look at it critically, and adapt more quickly to avoid these periods of stasis after accomplishment? And did it stem from the

IF I HAD $100.⁵ TO BET ON HER
OR ME, WHO WOULD I PUT IT ON?
                              -KR

#YourNextAct

way I grew up and experienced the world? As it would turn out, it did. Everything for me then came back to how we play. How play affects our creativity, innovation, and independent thought.

I grew up in a hands-off house. Outside of my mom's ten commandments, we did our own thing. It wouldn't be uncommon on a Saturday morning to make a bowl of Froot Loops mixed with chocolate chips, top it off with a side of barbecue chips and a can of orange pop. My dad was away working while Mom was busy cleaning and running the household. She'd wave us off in the morning, hollering, "See you at dinner!" Off we'd go on wild adventures in the forest.

Whenever I told my mother about something bugging me at school, instead of diagnosing the situation and telling me what I should do, she'd ask, "What do you think?" As a result, I became my own governor. I drew my own lines. When kids at school started drinking, sure, I drank, too. But I made my own decision about when to call it a night because my ethos, ethics, and integrity would come in—and that was more powerful than any potential punishment. Was this why I solved problems so well? I needed to know because here I was at the top. I was the one signing paychecks, and not checks for ten grand. These were checks for everything we owned. Everything was mortgaged, and anyone who has been involved in construction knows you can make a lot of money fast, but you can lose it just as fast. Besides, here I was, a twenty-eight-year-old woman running a construction company, not exactly the norm. Lest I ever forgot, there would always be someone to remind me. Like the guy who arrived for his interview and asked me to fetch him a coffee so he could watch my ass as I walked away to find my boss. "Yeah, I *am* the boss," I said. His face melted. He did not apologize, but I offered him the job anyway. What better person to work for you than one who feels he's done you wrong? He would do whatever I said now.

WHEN THE HOOPS DISAPPEAR

Now I was at the top and I owned my own company. There were fewer defined hoops to jump through, but in turn, the world became opaque. The closer you get to the top, the fewer people there are to tell you what to do, which is good and bad. After all, I spent a lot of time doing what was expected of me. A grand performance for which I should have won an Oscar. We all do it; we're all actors at some point in our lives and careers. We follow the script robotically instead of getting in tune with our character's ethos. Picture it, the point in the movie where everyone crowds around the star clapping and cheering and hoo-raying—but he's seeing it all in slow motion, thinking, "Why aren't I happy?" Most successful people have been in this place, and yet no one ever assumed they were unsatisfied, living unfulfilled lives.

We're smart people—we should know better. But by playing it safe, we've attached our own shackles. How do we get out?

BABY-STEPPING BACK INTO LIFE

I started with small adaptations. I had a certain way I drove to work, and always drove that way until one morning I took a new route. Here I am the boss lady, the woman who bases her whole day on productivity, wasting an extra five minutes. At restaurants, instead of ordering the same thing, I'd try something different. These were small and quiet steps. A practice that slowly broke me free from defaulting into a robotic, mechanical pattern. I was finding my voice again. I was making **choices** again.

The slow approach served me well. No one needed to know about these little changes except me. To declare something grandiose is to set yourself up. Consider someone going on an extreme diet. The second he caves on a small cookie, he figures he ruined the whole plan, so he may as well go back to his old ways and eat the whole damn pack.

The second part about the slow change is that it is low

risk. What's the threat of ordering a pâté over a plate of roasted beets? If I don't like it, I'll send it back and lose eleven bucks. The beautiful thing? The results are almost instant. When you engage with yourself for one small action out of your default, it feels like Freedom Town. The day I drove a different route to work, I felt lighter, my shackles slightly loosened. No one knew. But these baby steps allowed me to reengage with my life and start making choices in my life *and* work again, not just decisions at work.

I looked at every day as a chance to make an adaptation to my standard default. Soon, I found myself excited every morning—*what can I do differently today?*

DID YOU CHECK YOUR BLIND SPOT?

When we reach a stage of mastery in our field and people come to us with a problem or a problem presents itself, we make a decision. More often than not, it's obvious to us what the decision is, and feeling frustrated, we wonder how someone else couldn't have come up with the same conclusions when it's so *damn* obvious for us. It's knee jerk.

But with each decision comes a choice, and when you're making decisions all day, over time, you risk falling into a trap of believing you're always right (you often are, after all). But are you treating the array of choices presented to you fairly? Or are you mindlessly dismissing some—or even half of them? Think about it this way: when confronted with a problem, do you play out all the possibilities before coming to your decision? Do you allow your mind to wander down the darkly lit path, the dangerous one—the one some people might find a touch crazy?

There's a stark contrast between the decision for which we already know the answer and choices where we actually must consider more than one option as having potential. Just because you're a leader or a manager doesn't mean you're *choosing* things. A lot of times, those are just knee-jerk decisions, a result of our mastery. *But* how long does one's mastery remain fresh enough to allow a default response to the kind of decisions that ascend to the level of the leader?

Let's take an example. Let's say you're in a marketing meeting and someone presents a font as "the one." If asked why, he or she responds, "Because that's how it is," or, "Because it's the best one," or worse, "Because it's the one we've always used and we know the client likes it. Can we just move on?" Isn't it possible the client might like a different one even more? Does he or she have a choice anymore? As leaders, we must check our blind spots, the places where unexplored options lurk—these may be the hidden gems and are certainly the answers that didn't just come to us from muscle memory. When solving for X, are you just plugging in whatever is known? Let X remain unknown for a while and you may be surprised what you learn.

Back to our example with the font. Assume the junior staff wants to better understand why the specific font was "the one" and are now asking why our tenured expert believes he or she "just knows." If you're the tenured expert, you need to stop and ask yourself the same question: why? Maybe you haven't because you're afraid to truly question yourself, or to admit you've lost your edge, or that you no longer relate to millennials. Whatever it is, you can't let fear stop you from considering your choices. If there's something you get defensive about, you need to figure out why.

I want you—yes, you, the individual reading this book right now—to understand that it's actually because of your ascension, capacity, and ability. Your experience and history of making good, even *great* decisions, that when these things come up, it's as if there's a fork in the road with a light shining on your knee-jerk response answer. That instead of grabbing the glinting, glittery obvious, you allow yourself to be uncomfortable, to question your choices, and check your blind spot.

THE CALL

Ten years out of MBA school, I was giving my kids a bath when an old classmate called. "I saw you on the cover of a magazine and read you won Canada's number one female entrepreneur. And you know what?" He paused to chuckle and then said, "I never really thought you were that smart."

A lot of people would have been pissed off to hear such a thing, but it actually brought me joy. It reminded me about how we define success. I'd beaten myself up for so long about not being good or smart enough, and none of those skills had anything to do with success as I define it, because there's so much that school can't teach. But what he said also sparked a question: why me and not him? Three hundred and eighty Western MBA graduates headed out into the big bad world the year I graduated, yet all 380 are not at the top. Why? With my own self-deprecating nature, I had to ask, how did I wind up at the top?

There is no ROI that we can calculate based on the time and money spent on a certain path. Having an MBA improved my odds but didn't guarantee a thing. It was through my research about how play opens our minds and sets the stage for innovation that reminded me of my youthful escapades in the forest. The bliss that came with living life unabashed. It reminded me what I do best and that I needed to do it again. "I'm not going to play small anymore," I told myself. "This is legit. It wasn't all luck. I am clever." It was the rocket fuel for the next adaptation. I broke completely free from my shackles, and the next year, I won Canada's Entrepreneur award again.

If my life was a Hollywood movie, this would be a great place to end. Hurrah, our underdog proved them all wrong and got to the top! But I wasn't ready to call "cut" on my own life. Who is? The reality of winning the award for a second, consecutive year was that I had to face all these people who had now set even higher expectations for me, all of them asking, "What's new? What's next?"

The record scratches, the candy-colored confetti pauses in midair, the balloons deflate. What's next?

It's like standing on top of a mountain you'd worked your life to climb to find you have two options:

1. Sit down and enjoy the view from there, period.
2. Admit to yourself that simply being on top isn't enough, although beautiful. The view will begin to bore you. You secretly want to climb another mountain.
3. Which would you want to do? Stay in the static of that accomplishment, or perhaps try it again a little differently?

Now what? How do I follow my own act? It's like a *Choose Your Own Adventure* book and there are two routes. If you want to stay at the party well after all the people you like have left and the party fizzles out completely, don't turn the page. If you want to go find a new party, turn the page. What do you want to do?

If only life were so explicative, right? Because this is a book, I will be—here's where you turn the page.

Chapter 2

UNINTENTIONAL OBSOLESCENCE

Our minds are wired to grow. When we were young, our minds were constantly engaged because everything was new. With each passing year, we become more specialized in our fields. And specialization can be dangerous in that it narrows our focus. By the time we're in our thirties and forties, we have greatly prohibited our minds from doing what they do best, because we stay at the comfortable party until we're bored out of our wits but too afraid to leave.

Everyone has felt the rush of meeting a new friend with a similar interest, or finding amazing new music, or reading about an incredible job opportunity. We only got the rush from broadening our horizon. The fundamental essence of becoming exceptional and futureproofing stems from the notion that you need to stock your mental shelves with new resources for new outcomes. There's beauty in the butterflies. When your stomach flutters, it means you're actively engaged and invested in the moment. Butterflies are a great indicator that your mind does not know what's about to happen next—and that's vital. It means you shed from your default shackles; you might even get wings.

TWO TYPES OF HIGH ACHIEVERS, BOTH STUCK

Let's look at two different types of people, each an achiever. First, we've got the underdogs, who despite the odds, make it big. Often, they're more daring because they're dragon chasers after the next high. Dragon chasers get stuck when the highs (in other words, their successes and awards) become shallow and meaningless. I don't mean the person has become shallow or that the awards became any less difficult to win, but because every high must be exceeded.

Our second group consists of the smarties, those we predicted would succeed. They check boxes like nobody's business and often excel at buying into the game. Which one are you? We know there are two totally different people with totally different approaches, yet they're equally as likely to stagnate. But why?

How Do You FEEL WHEN You HAVE
REACHED THE TOP AND You WERE
BORN TO CLIMB?
　　　　　　　　　-KR

Your NextAct

CAN'T GET NO SATISFACTION

Consider the world in the 1950s. One's view was limited to whatever was available in the neighborhood, the newspaper, and the radio. Throw in the occasional *National Geographic* and that's all, folks. We had far less to compare ourselves against and didn't miss out on what we didn't know existed. Today's reach has expanded exponentially and brought a new competitive edge. What was once reserved for superheroes is now reality. It's us against the world. As a result, our attention spans have shifted. How many news articles could someone read in the 1950s compared to today? We're up against the impossible. We cannot read it all. We cannot know it all. There's so much happening that it's harder for us to focus on longer, richer pursuits.

Consequently, our value sets changed. Today's "more" is a hell of a lot more than it was in the 1950s, so what will tomorrow's "more" be? Less? More than we can imagine? We don't know and that's why we get scared. When I was in high school, I didn't know 80 percent of the jobs that were out there. Hell, I didn't know much outside Kelowna, British Columbia, because guess why? I didn't have the World Wide Web. I had my friends, my family, and MTV. Today's high schoolers have a lot more, and because of that, it's more difficult to feel satiated. That's not to say we're all afflicted with depression, rather that the world we're comparing ourselves against expanded to the degree to which we can't help but feel lesser than.

In the past, our friends generally saved their bragging rights for the annual holiday letter. Suzy got accepted to Harvard and Jimmy is first chair saxophone! Today, the bragging rights are constant. We're overdosed with our friends' photos and best selves displayed, pushed—shoved into our faces from social media. Unsurprisingly, we then think, "Shit, I better post something amazing today, too!"

The same goes for feedback in our careers. Years ago, the boss might tell you you're doing OK at the annual party. Since that time, human resources procedures kicked in and we got an annual review. Somehow, that annual review turned into quarterly reviews and then into daily huddles—and for some, hourly reminders. There's feedback galore. We're judged constantly or constantly seeking shorter term validation, both narrowing and shortening our focus to the point that it's difficult to gain clarity on what we want when we can't see past our noses or the next accolade to hit.

THE STEP FUNCTION MODEL

In the past, we treated our satisfaction as a step function. In mathematical terms, a step function is like sets of stairs. The first set goes up. It flattens and another set begins. We graduate from high school (step up), we go on our way for a bit (flatland), we get a job or additional training (step up). Every time we stepped up, there was enough space to get traction. Today, the steps come on much faster. The time in between doesn't have as much traction, and the stairs themselves are not clearly defined. We cling to what's comfortable—the norms. In my case, go to university, get an MBA, check the boxes, win an award, and then what? Back on the flatland, but now it's sticky, and there are no stairs in sight. Once we get so high, there's no one left to build another step for us. It's up to us to get out our tools and build one, but instead, we stagnate. We assume we need permission to build the next step. Or it's risky because it doesn't come with a lick of instructions. Or now that we are up here, everyone is watching and perhaps they don't agree with the next stair; it's not what they would have predicted for me. Why do we feel this way? We're sovereign adults! Because we were trained that way. We're those smart seals at the show doing the tricks just for the fish. We go through training and we check our checklist; now, how do we differentiate ourselves from all the other well-trained seals?

We must recognize when we've plateaued and build our next steps instead of waiting for them to appear. To build new steps, we must make daily adaptations away from our defaulted norm. Don't categorize the step-up in this metaphor to mean only a step up a corporate ladder or a financial increase; this step is more like man's first step on the moon—it may feel small at first, but it's a giant leap toward becoming exceptional. But you do have to take that step. You must alter your life's default recipe, or you'll never lift off.

Care to do the work? Check out the exercise titled Step Function Model in the back of the book.

INSATIABLE ACQUISITIONS

Imagine a stream with two forks in it. The fork creates two tracks for the stream to travel down. One track leads toward a physical acquisition punctuated by an emotional charge. The other leads toward an experiential acquisition punctuated by an emotional change. People tend to favor one of these tracks over the other.

The first track leads toward acquisition—as in acquiring a piece of paper from school or a new car; it always leads to something tangible. It's a home or a husband, or whatever it is you're aiming to acquire. There's a clear line in the sand for the goal and reaching it.

What I've witnessed from people who are extremely driven or ambitious is an innate drive to acquire something, to outwardly achieve or accomplish something. These people will say, "I got the degree; now I need the house. I got the house; now I need the [enter the next upgrade here]."

WE ARE SOVERIGN ADULTS.

-KR

#YourNextAct

The churn of acquisition is insatiable. It's not that those yearning to acquire are constantly hungry for something bigger or more expensive. It's more the act of the hunt that keeps them going. It's the pursuit of the chase.

The other track leads toward an experiential response. Those on this track may be chasing or running from a goal to satisfy an emotional need only. It could be worthiness or fitting in, or a host of other formidable emotions. These people are driven in a different way than those aiming to acquire, but the pursuit is similar in that it's the chase to do or accomplish something they consider makes them "better." Consider it this way: for those riding along this track, it's more about the emotion that comes with graduating than it is the tangible piece of paper.

SUCKERS FOR PUNISHMENT

Recently, I was speaking with a highly accomplished fellow who has traveled the world speaking and giving workshops on negotiation. At eighty years old, he's no longer asking himself what his act two is—he's on act seven; and when he crushes act seven, he's going to move on to act eight. What he told me was this: "No matter what amount of therapy I could take to make me happy, it comes down to this: I've done it all. I've done all the personal work. I've walked over the coals and yet,

I'll always be chasing that feeling of accomplishment and worthiness."

It struck me why: it brought both folks of the stream back together. Whether acquiring things or experiences, it might be that the reason we, the ambitious, keep coming back for "more" even once we've achieved our goals. It's that perhaps it's in the discomfort of pursuit that the ambitious feel most comfortable.

Do you know someone (and maybe it's you) who messes things up just when they get great? It's like solving the Rubik's Cube and immediately dismantling it because the high of reaching the end goal lasts only so long.

I need to feel like I'm either on track one—acquiring and working toward an acquisition—or track two—feeling as though I'm working toward having that high or comfort. Of course, it's slightly different for everyone, but for me, it's so freeing. For some, it's stasis and warmth. I can't claim what exactly it should feel like for you, but recognize that the discomfort of pursuit is where we're most comfortable because without it, we're neither going to acquire anything further nor have that sense of self for which we yearn—momentary as it may be. It's rarely about the end moment; it's almost always about the process. And so, it's no wonder that when we get to *the moment*, and we're on the other side of our goal, that we

SOMETIMES THE DISCOMFORT OF
PURSUIT IS WHERE THE AMBITIOUS
FEEL MOST COMFORTABLE.
                                    -KR

Your Next Act

feel empty. We don't yet have the next process figured out, and that level of discomfort is far more uncomfortable than the discomfort of a challenging pursuit.

When what we have mastered becomes mundane, we feel pain. The antidote is pursuit.

THE NEED TO REFINE OUR LANGUAGE

We all speak more than one language, even if you're not bilingual—just stay with me. English may be your first language, and it's what you use to construct sentences understood by others who speak English. You speak another language, too. Maybe even a third or fourth. These secondary and tertiary languages are your specialties; they're like a lens, and they determine how you see the world and interpret it for others.

Albert Einstein was feeling particularly frustrated with his work one day. So he got out of the office to ride his bike around the park. As he rode, he observed the world around him and noted how a stationary park bench appeared to be in motion in relation to a second stationary object—a tree. The perception totally changed his perspective. Excited, he returned to his office to tell the first person he found about it, and from there began work on the theory of relativity via his transformative emotional experience.

When Einstein fully worked out the theory of relativity, he used his second language to explain it; physics was his second language. Maybe your specialized language is neural science or care and compassion. MBA school gave me a business language, just as it did for a whole slew of folks. I differentiate myself from all the people who also speak fluent business with my third language: human connection. If my language is confined to business acumen only, and I'm not able to translate my skillset to those outside that world, I'll never be exceptional in my pursuits—the things *I* want to do, the things that drive *me*. My reach will be narrowed. I need to enhance my vocabulary to transcend languages. We'll talk more about how to become more relevant, alive, and interesting in chapter 4, but an easy example of expanding your language's reach and intrigue is by reading a magazine outside your interest every month. If I read *Field & Stream* magazine, I add new words to my vocabulary. I don't know when they'll be useful, but I'm stocking my shelves in preparation. Let's be clear: I'm not acquiring fish vocabulary; I am exposing myself to new information, outside of my language. Business ain't fish. By constantly enriching our vocabulary and collecting new ingredients, we're preparing our language to be understood by people and companies from all places, specializations, and backgrounds. Consider two finance experts with the same education, but one of them is also fluent in marketing; he's got that marketing lens to look through. The additional marketing language makes him more valuable than his counterpart.

We learned our first language after birth, and we developed a second language through training. But unless we expand our experiences, we're not doing our second and third languages justice, and we certainly aren't learning a new one. When we're not adapting from our status quo, our vocabulary suffers, and our anecdotes suck. We're parrots repeating the same thing, which makes us predictable, boring, and obsolete.

WHAT IS OUR BIGGEST MISTAKE?

Ken Robinson's TED Talk addresses how the traditional school system kills creativity. He dispels the idea that obtaining a certain level of expertise readies us. "Ready" is what keeps us small, stuck, and very much at risk of becoming rapidly irrelevant to ourselves. After winning Canada's Top Female Entrepreneur award for the second time and waking up to feel dread for a year and a half, it was because I was no longer relevant to my own life. I got comfortable and stopped building steps. When three-star Michelin chef Alain Passard decided to take his restaurant in a new direction, one that focused on vegetables, it was because he internally felt that sense of dread, that his dishes were no longer relevant. And even if they were still relevant to the crowd, how long would that last if he didn't feel that way himself? There is no way to create a positive impact around us when we internally feel irrelevant. Passard admitted to himself what he felt, he addressed it, and he adapted his routine. The results were nothing short of exceptional.

Stephen Hawking said, "The greatest enemy of knowledge is not ignorance; it's the illusion of knowledge." When we reach the top or even a "good enough" place, we stop exploring. That's dangerous. That's our hypothetical vanilla cake baker assuming the world will forever want vanilla cake. He didn't plan on becoming obsolete—none of us do—but he didn't take any steps to prevent it either. He specialized in a skill that allowed him to maintain his top position for a notable amount of time. But by maintaining his position and stocking only quality vanilla, he wasn't progressing. Maintenance, even if at the top of the scale, results in a diminishing pay grade over time. When the world decides it prefers blueberry streusel to vanilla cake, our vanilla cake baker's maintenance efforts are left in the dust.

What if the reigning Olympic gold medalist in women's all-around gymnastics returned to the next Olympic Games with all the same routines? It doesn't mean the value of all the moves isn't incredible, but without innovation, it's lackluster and its value has decreased enormously. What makes you valuable in the future is your ability to come up with new and innovative thoughts. Doing the same, albeit great, work you've already done is your standard and won't move you forward.

Why are you reading this book? You picked it up for some reason. My guess is because your default future is not ideal. Let's get really personal now.

WHAT'S YOUR PROBLEM?

Are you fantasizing or dreaming? Whatever funk you're in, will it pass in a few months, or will it linger until you do something about it? In other words, stop and gut-check. Is it a dream or a fantasy that's haunting you? Remember, the dream will endure the inconvenient, but the fantasy will fizzle.

Next question: if you had a conversation with your dream opportunity, what would it sound like? What would you say to it? "Crap, you got here too soon. I'm not ready!" Or maybe, "May I please have the checklist for launch?" You may find a lot of excuses because you see a lot of problems: I don't have enough money. I don't have enough time. I don't have the right connections. I don't [insert problem here]. So now what? You're not chasing your dream because you don't know what will happen if you do? I hate to point out the obvious, but you don't know what's going to happen no matter *what* you do. No one does. You don't need to solve your dream overnight. You just need to build momentum with small, baby steps.

If you don't start making even small adaptations in your life now, when will you? The truth is, likely never. How does that sit? You can break from your default, screw stagnation, and come back to feeling driven and alive **right now**. Are you going to do it, or are you just going to sit there and let the future do its own damn thing? Maybe read another book and hope that by osmosis things get better. Well, maybe I took that too far, too harsh, but can we agree that we have to *do* something different for something to change?

WHERE DO I START?

Write down your pain points. These should be the aspects from your life that you want to eliminate from your default future. Your pain points may fall on a spectrum from your entire career to the ten pounds you wish to lose. Write them all down and don't stress. This is a cathartic exercise, not a test. You won't lose points by scratching things out, forgetting some, or adding more later. Like the futureproofing process, these will evolve. If you're feeling stuck, ask yourself, "Given the choice, would I endure [enter pain point here] forever?"

When you have your list, prioritize the pain points by

urgency. Start with the easiest, lowest-hanging fruit with the highest sense of urgency. The scale of urgency is different for everyone and depends on individual pain tolerance.

Give it a go with the exercise: What I Do Not Want. It's best paired with solitude, great music in the background, and perhaps a scotch.

Do you think the world's best athletes trained without having to endure physical pain? That their coaches told them they were doing an awesome job every day? Of course not. To improve, we must be willing to take the constructive discomfort. Maybe you're willing to take the harsh words from a trainer in the gym before you hear them from your boss or staff? I don't know you and can't tell you how you feel. Decide. Circle those aspects of your life and career that are like a slow-growing cancer. Then admit it's there. The cancer itself does not kill the organism; it's the cancer's impact on vital functions that kills the host. Perhaps alone, the pain points will not kill your career or spirit directly, but their impact on your vital functions will be your demise. Admitting you have something worth addressing is the first stage in treatment.

Some discomfort may feel akin to a poke in the ass, while addressing pain points may make slamming your hand in a door look like a good time. As for urgency, extreme

ADAPTATION DOSN'T ALWAYS FEEL
GOOD. THERE WILL BE A LEVEL OF
CONSTRUCTIVE DISCOMFORT. — KR

Your NextAct

health issues rise to the top, or if your job is in jeopardy (and you want to save it), that's obviously high on the urgency scale. Whichever way you tackle your pain points, remember that you won't futureproof yourself into exceptionalism overnight; the key is to take small, consistent steps and build momentum.

Even on paper, your smallest pain points may look overwhelming because you've allowed them to exist on the horizon. Once you reach out and grab one, you may be surprised to see how small it is. Grab one at a time. If one of your less urgent desires is to gain more professional connections, your strategy can be as simple as inviting someone out for coffee and starting a new conversation. That first baby step is like picking up a weight; you develop your muscles a little bit more each day. If you don't, you're not getting stronger. You're stagnating. And if you want another way of looking at what stagnation does in the long term, consider the way traditional Chinese medicine defines it: where there is stagnation, there is pain and sickness.

If you don't start with even your easiest pain point, you're still influencing your future. By not making a choice, you're making one, because life will go on with or without your next move. It doesn't feel good to admit, but you can use it to your advantage. Few things are more motivating than when you make moves that will directly affect your

WHERE THERE IS STAGNATION, THERE
IS PAIN AND SICKNESS — CHINESE PROVERB

Your Next Act

future. That's why kids' lives are so motivating. We never look at them and say, "Hey, little fella, you're fine where you are. Just settle! Forget that whole reaching-for-the-stars nonsense." Why talk to ourselves that way? Let's take it even further and consider this: would you still be friends with someone if he talked to you the way you talk to yourself? Pull to mind the worst things you've ever told yourself, your lowest moments. Would a friend say that to you? "You're a big fat failure, a real sack of shit. What the hell did you even do today?" If so, hopefully you're not friends with him or her anymore. You get the point. Give yourself a break. Try to be your own friend.

Start collecting new ingredients with the easiest, lowest-hanging fruit. What's the easiest change you can make today? Can you walk a new route home or go to a new restaurant, speak to a stranger on the train? Yes, you can and you will. Or you won't, and you'll stay where you are.

WHAT'S YOUR DEFAULT FUTURE?

If you don't make any adaptations, if you stay right where you are, what does your future look like? Are you OK with it? If the answer is no, let's keep moving.

Book Two

———

ADDRESS IT

Chapter 3

WHAT MAKES YOU VALUABLE IN THE FUTURE?

It's easy to define how we were valuable in the past. When we consider the future, it's a lot more difficult to know where we'll fit in, how we'll be relevant, and what will make us valuable—even what makes us feel most alive. The idea around futureproofing is not that you make yourself bulletproof—that's not possible. Life gives us highs and lows, and we still have feelings. We may be trying to outsmart robots to save our jobs, but we don't want to become them, right?

The key to futureproofing yourself is to enhance your ability to adapt. Adaptation requires an open mind. We have to be nimble to keep evolving. We are not the same people we were ten years ago. It's systemic—somewhere in our thirties and forties, we slow toward a full stop of adapting.

We must relieve ourselves from the traditional thinking that a knowledge subset is what defines our value. My subset? I have my MBA, I've won some awards, and I'm a good mom. These are good indicators of my future potential insofar as they increase the probability I'll deliver a positive outcome, but there's no guarantee. By default, we automatically go to the checklist instead of incorporating the whole of our knowledge base, which includes our experiences and our openness. What creates value in a person is much broader, and you know it. As uncomfortable as it is to not rely on the boxes checked, what creates exceptional value in a person is never in a box. It's **never** in a box.

ALL NEW THINGS ARE TWO PREVIOUSLY UNCONNECTED THOUGHTS

Nothing comes from space. If I ask you to create something with whatever you find in your fridge right now, what will you come up with? What would your neighbor create? Your boss? Creating a dish that's deliciously memorable will take more than box-checking. Alain Passard, our risk-taking French chef, never wrote a single recipe. He knows one can never perfectly recreate the past, and why would he want to? He's an innovator. He adapts to the produce delivered to his restaurant every day, and how refreshing is that? I doubt he wakes with dread. A predictable, box-checking day is what causes dread for

IT'S NEVER IN A BOX.
— KR

Your Next Act

people like us, you and me. Innovations come to those who constantly adapt. Remember, stagnation is a sickness, which if left unchecked, may result in death.

The second reason why we must adapt is because of how quickly the world is changing. It took sixty years for most people to adopt a landline telephone into their homes. Think about that! You had sixty years to consider if the thing was right for you. The smartphone? It took only three to five years depending on the country. Compare the adaptation curve in the past to a train that came through town once a day. The train rested at the station for a couple of hours and the conductor always shouted, "All aboard" long before he ignited a painfully slow start out of town. You can picture it, right? The kind of train you could jog after and still effortlessly board. When you do, you lean out of the car's door and tip your hat to those who stayed at the station.

Technology, globalization, and our thirst for "better and more" changed the adaptation curve to move like a high-speed train. This train moves so quickly that if you take a second to consider boarding or not, the train's gone. The more you miss, the further behind you fall. We don't want to be waiting around for the next train, aka the flip-phone person forever justifying why she doesn't have a smartphone.

Here's where we tend to ask where the future train is

going, because despite how intelligent we are, we still want to know the future. While I don't have a crystal ball, I can say that my train is not headed for more training. I'm not going to do another MBA. I might take the occasional brush-up course, but to be truly exceptional, I need more experiences. That's where I have the greatest ability to obtain more tools to explain in my special language(s) what's new and insightful. And even when people tell me I'm doing great and that I'm succeeding, I must move forward. I can't get off at the station to relish in my accomplishments, because the moment I do, I become a little less relevant. I miss a train.

Our brain wakes every morning and says, "What's next? Where are we headed?" Outsmarting obsolescence doesn't mean we should be the first person into the office every day with the latest and greatest app, citing world news to the minute. Like a crash diet, it's not realistic, because it's not sustainable. We outsmart obsolescence by remaining nimble and making small adaptations every day.

THE X GENE

Adaptation is like a mutant gene that becomes central to survival. However, it is not until the mutation is brought into the world that a species knows how it's useful. From the outside, we may view a successful mutation and aspire to achieve what it has been able to do. Over time, the hot new mutation becomes the expectation, and back to the beginning we go.

We humans only want to adapt our behavior if we know what the outcome will be. We want to ask the future to vet our mutations, tell us what species will be valuable before we make any moves. Life doesn't work that way. If we waited to mutate until after the market assured us the mutation was successful, it's too late. Our survival is at risk. Stop wasting your time presupposing what mutation you need to evolve. All you need to do is keep adapting, try a few things out, and when the adaptation becomes useful, you will know it.

WHY YOU CAN'T TRUST THE WORLD

The world may tell you you're doing great, but if you don't feel it, is it true? None of us wants to feel like we're simply keeping up. We want to remain at the head of the pack.

Remember, you are driven and ambitious. You were born wired that way, so what works for most simply does not work for you.

Consider your rate of becoming obsolete in physics terms. Momentum in physics is mass times velocity ($p = mv$). Velocity is speed and direction. The larger something is, the more embedded it is and the more mass it has. Direction simply refers to what's happening.

To change an entire team's productivity or attitude is not easy. That's why large organizations, ones with enormous mass, struggle to adapt. The good news? We are not the company we work for anymore, and we as individuals are able to adapt much faster than an overarching organization. Your mass? It's just you. You're not trying to affect eight hundred other people or an entire silo of work. As for the direction you're heading? Unless you're doing something, you don't have much direction. All you need to do is start.

If you in fact are trying to move an organization—heck, if you are driven to change the world—let's refer to that clever chap Gandhi. "Be the change you want to see." It still starts with you.

When we want to stop ourselves from traveling in a bad direction, we rely on methods that worked in the past. Those methods may slow our trajectory, but they won't switch our direction. A corporation has a large mass, and therefore, it's exponentially more difficult to halt the ship. So the company plays it safe and makes very small adaptations. Consequently, the company's outcome won't be significant in the shorter term, whereas even a small adaptation made by an individual (with much smaller mass) will have a noticeable effect. As such, corporations benefit when they start at the individual level. They should take the time to help each person adapt and improve. In the long run, this will change their course for the better. Unfortunately, most corporations overlook individuals and attempt to move the whole ship at once.

Most corporations also look to the competitive landscape for cues and integrate what they see working well. In our own lives, instead of integrating and adapting, we focus on what we're good at and integrate what worked in the past. If we want to futureproof ourselves and have a positive effect in the mass-times-velocity conversation, we must keep collecting ingredients. They provide both speed and direction when stocked correctly, allowing for a meaningful and masterful combination at pace. But we will get to exactly how to do that.

WANT TO PLAY A GAME?

Think of an experience. Do it right now. Got it? I'm willing to bet that the experience was one that fell outside your defaulted norm. Maybe you thought of a travel destination or a frightening roller coaster. Humans recall experiences when they're tied to an emotional alteration. We pay attention when we engage our emotions. Have you ever driven home only to arrive and wonder how you got there? We've all been victims of highway hypnosis. Sure, we were there for the drive, but we can't recall a moment of it. We must call our minds to attention the way a drill sergeant calls to his team. Otherwise, we're living our life in a state of highway hypnosis. What an absolute downright bore! Who would put up with it? What will you remember? What will you experience living that way? Our minds are simply not designed to remember, if they're not engaged emotionally—it's a scientific fact. Mary Helen Immordino-Yang explains in her book *Emotions, Learning, and the Brain*, "It is literally neurobiologically impossible to build memories, engage complex thoughts, or make meaningful decisions without emotion. And after all, this makes sense: the brain is highly metabolically expensive tissue, and evolution would not support wasting energy and oxygen thinking about things that don't matter to us. Put succinctly, we only think about things we care about."

I bet I could quiz my colleagues from MBA school by asking them to recite the theorem behind any of the many strategic models we learned, and they'd get the first part right before having to resort to a book. How many studying sessions are memorable for the long haul? Experiences must have emotion attached to become unforgettable.

A DISCLAIMER

I'm not sure this is the right time to tell you this, but I'm not done with this book—by that I mean, the work isn't finished. I've spent my life leading into this understanding and the last three and a half years trying to capture it into words so I could share it with you. This book, as in the writing of this passage, has been fully complete and sitting on my desk for seven months, waiting for me to green-light the first print.

The reason it sat for seven months is because it's not done; my thinking on the subject, deeper discoveries, and rich conversations are still to be had, which will only add more to our understanding.

I called a great friend, coach, and colleague a month ago and told her the problem with the book—that despite my being tremendously proud of it, I could not press Play because I know there is more.

Perfectly, she asked me which author of ideas and discoveries ever wrote the perfect preeminent work in one volume, printed it, and threw his or her hands in the air resounding, "My work here is done!"

None.

Zero.

Zilch.

So I want to be clear that this work is not done; it's a hell of a long way down the track, and I've gathered riches of insight and understanding every era along the way. But this last part...well, it's on me to get this book out to start the bigger, broader conversation. To deepen, enrich, and of course, adapt.

There will be a volume 2, and that's where you come in. So pay damn close attention because this is where the book gets good *and* involves you, should you want to become part of the exploration.

I openly admitted at the beginning that I'm not a scientist, researcher, or guru; I am a person, like you, who discovered a few gifts, had successes, and reached paramount moments, yet wondered, *Is there more*, and *How do I feel this again?* How do I become futureproof from success to success? And that's exactly what I will show you next, what I have learned to date, and I know there's more. But this is where we begin.

MENTAL SHELF REAL ESTATE

Imagine everything you know and remember as if it were stocked on a bookshelf. Your brain is fed information constantly and must determine what to store on those shelves and keep for the long term. There are three ways through which the brain will vet information to store onto your shelves:

1. Training: what we're taught (it's in a book)
2. Experience: unknown outcome (individualized)
3. Emotional attachment: our personal exploration of an experience

We know there's a ton of information stored on our mental shelves. Naturally, we create a hierarchy with them. We favor one shelf over the other because it helps us navigate more quickly. But consider what happens when you favor one muscle over the other? If you lift weights with only your right arm, your left arm becomes flabby and dull. You do not want your brain to become flabby and dull. Your brain is plastic and willing to adapt and rewire throughout your entire lifetime. If you don't work it out properly, however, it won't do its job.

From *Neuroplasticity: Learning Physically Changes the Brain* by Sara Bernard via Edutopia.com:

> According to neurologist and educator Judy Willis (and suggested by a research-rich chapter in the second edition of *Developmental Psychopathology*, among many other publications), neuroplasticity is defined as the selective organizing of connections between neurons in our brains.

This means that when people repeatedly practice an activity or access a memory, their neural networks—groups of neurons that fire together, creating electrochemical pathways—shape themselves according to that activity or memory. When people stop practicing new things, the brain will eventually eliminate, or "prune," the connecting cells that formed the pathways. Like in a system of freeways connecting various cities, the more cars going to certain destinations, the wider the road that carries them needs to be. The fewer cars traveling that way, however, the fewer lanes are needed.

The shelf you favor is your eye-level shelf; it's the most expensive real estate because it gets drawn from the most often just as the eye-level shelf does in a grocery store. Everyone knows that in real estate, it's all about location, location, location; the same goes for your brain. You access your prime real estate, your eye-level shelf, so often that it becomes your most frequently traveled neural pathway. Your eye-level shelf is filled with the information and memories you reference most often. The more often you use it, the more prominent it becomes, and consequently, your other shelves fizzle into unreachable areas. Following a routine and living on autopilot are the greatest contributors to stocking your eye-level shelf and those nearest to it with mundane ingredients. Pulling from only this shelf also serves to isolate the eye-level shelf from the rest of your mind's knowledge. Think about how wasteful that is—to let all those other shelves go unused and all those ingredients go stale.

Yes. Stale.

THE 3E MODEL

The 3E Model requires you to engage in a new experience, that the experience elicits an emotional response, and that you embed the memory permanently, as a new ingredient for your mental shelves, by verbally sharing the experience with another human. We'll cover the 3E Method further in chapter 6. Just remember these three easy Es:

1. **Experience**: engaging in experience
2. **Emotion**: an experience-related emotional response
3. **Embed**: communicating the experience with another human being

PRESCRIBING 3E

When you follow a routine and live in a rut, you aren't tapping into your potential. You are predictable. To rise to exceptionalism, you must not only strategically stock eye-level shelves but also incorporate *all* your mental shelves and—this is the crucial part—you must keep expanding them. That requires you to make small adaptations from your default routine every day.

When you make adaptations from your default routine, you exercise your other mental shelves and you store new ingredients. Make those adaptions; keep your brain active, respect it. It has the power to make you exceptional.

YOUR TOOLS ARE OUTDATED

We need experiences that fall outside of our knowledge subset. Our knowledge subset is that eye-level shelf from which we grab because it's right in front of us. It's so easy. It's the stuff we've specialized in, what we know in our sleep. An innovator's shelves are stocked with diverse ingredients, because they constantly add more. Additionally, they step on the stool to reach their top shelves as easily and effortlessly as they crouch down to reach the lower shelves.

How do you expand your shelves? You may be thinking you should just go out and do a bunch of stuff. No. Go back to those questions we talked about in the last chapter about your list of pain points and their urgency. Make small adaptations away from your default to address the pain points and start with the easiest.

Along with my language, what differentiates me from the other MBA graduates are my experiences. We become unintentionally obsolete by focusing narrowly on one expertise. We think it makes us more applicable, but the diminishing returns will kick in at a certain point. One more incremental level of knowledge doesn't necessarily add one full unit of value. If life is a battlefield (life, not love—this is not a Pat Benatar metaphor) and we notice all the cannons shooting in one spot but avoiding another, we'll probably go to the safe spot and want to stay there. Let's think of the playing-it-safe spot as our existing knowledge. The reality is, our safe spot won't last forever, so let's get active and keep moving. To be exceptional, you need to be an exception to your own rule.

One sure sign the world is changing comes with Ernst & Young's decision to no longer require an MBA for senior management positions. They recognized the old model was broken and stopped to ask themselves what type of person they really wanted to hire. People who can read a book and regurgitate things? Or leaders and innovators? When a company of this size breaks the mold, it tells us what our safeguarded training means. An MBA alone isn't going to cut it. This doesn't just apply to MBA and business but nearly all training. Recall that if it can be taught, it can be programmed. Robots versus renegades. Or robots versus renegades with strategic experience. Who will win?

To be exceptional, you need to be an exception to your own rule.

— KR

THE TIME IT TAKES TO LEARN SOMETHING NEW IS ABBREVIATED

When I discovered the band Nirvana, I was the coolest kid in school because I was a fan a year before they hit the scene hard. Word spread, and I was the go-to gal for mixtapes. I could have kept serving Green Day and Nirvana tapes long after they became mainstream, but in doing so, I would have unintentionally become obsolete. To stay on top, I would have had to constantly search for what was next. Back then, I had a few months to stay alive with my mixtapes, whereas with today's rate of change, all it would take is a day. The more days you let slide, the more unintentionally obsolete you become because it becomes increasingly more difficult to catch up.

PRESS YES TO ACCEPT THE LATEST UPGRADE

Consider a window treatment designer. She's feeling stuck in her career, like she's making the same thing over and over again. So she decides to do more training. Chances are, many in her field will do the same. Sure, the training is a form of upgrading, but it's more like your phone asking you if you want to download the latest upgrade. Everyone does it, so how is your phone any different? It's not an *up*grade; it's an equalization for the driven.

What if the window treatment designer takes the

additional training but then travels in search of new experiences. While in Vietnam, she notices how local architects applied materials to a building, not even a window. Maybe the materials are installed at an interesting angle, and she has an aha moment. She thinks their method could be applied to window treatments. She connects the design with one of her standard designs to innovate and create something no one else has done before. In other words, she took her known ingredient (one everyone had access to) and combined it with a new and unexpected one. Without the trip to Vietnam (which could have been any new experience that involved an emotional alteration), she would still be hanging around the eye-level shelf using her same old spices. Instead, she pushed herself into the future. And as we've talked about, she can't stop there if she wants to go on being exceptional.

To bring the window treatment designer example to life, call an architect to mind. Any architect. Who did you think of? For most, it's Frank Lloyd Wright and for good reason. He's considered the greatest architect of the twentieth century. Let's look at his approach. Wright cut his traditional educational training short when he dropped out of the University of Wisconsin. He didn't fully check that box. Next, he moved to Chicago to apprentice at the world-renowned architectural firm Adler & Sullivan. Given their pick between a diploma and a chance to intern at this firm, I'd bet any sum that most architects would choose the latter.

After a few solid years of apprenticing, Wright opened his own firm in the Chicago suburb of Oak Park. The prairie design he's so known for started here, an inspiration from the prairies and rolling hills of his childhood in Spring Green, Wisconsin. The organic design and flat lines presented a stylistic disruption amid the classic Victorian homes surrounding Wright's own home and studio (where today tens of thousands tour each year) and his first, early adapter commissioned projects. The Europeans were far quicker to adapt to his style. Like the landline phone, Chicagoans took their time before determining if Wright's eccentric style held merit. Eventually, they hopped on his train, and then it picked up its pace. Soon, it seemed there were as many Wright or Wright-influenced designed homes in Oak Park as were Victorian homes.

Great, he could stop here, right? Sure, but Frank Lloyd Wright was an innovator, so he didn't. He expanded his ingredients and tools, stocking one during a visit to the World's Fair of 1893 held in Chicago, which would prove monumental throughout his career. It was here that Wright fell in love with Japanese art, a passion recognized today as a major force in his aesthetic inspiration. Still, he didn't stop with the exhibit. He traveled to Japan several times (he would later open an office in Tokyo during his work on the Imperial Hotel) and even sold Japanese block prints to his American and European clientele on the side.

Wright could have clung to his prairie-style homes for the remainder of his career, or at least to pay the bills (although many who have done business with him will tell you he did not pay his bills), but he didn't. Wright innovated until his death. He went on to design the Usonian home (better known today as the ranch home), the architectural masterpiece Fallingwater, and the only building to withstand the Great Kantō earthquake of 1923.

Frank Lloyd Wright was a master ingredient collector who knew innovations didn't happen at the desk. And that the second he started playing it safe, he'd no longer be exceptional—first to the world, foremost to himself.

HAVE I STOPPED COLLECTING INGREDIENTS?

What was the last ingredient you stocked onto your shelf? Remember, an ingredient is a new experience, tool, or even a person. An ingredient enriches your knowledge and perspective. I often ask my clients to draw a timeline of their lives and mark down the notable events. As you can imagine, there are a lot in the early years and a gradual deceleration as the timeline goes on. What are you collecting? Check out the exercise called Ingredients on Your Mental Shelf in the Exercises section of the book to find out.

In part, this is because we tend to note less of our experiences over time, but the primary reason is because as we age, we tend to develop experience rigor mortis—dead to anything new; essentially, we close ourselves off from new experiences. We stop observing the world, or when we do, we judge the hell out of it. This rigor mortis experience makes us stiff, and as a result, we don't even come in contact with anything notable unless it's forced on us.

Most people assume that we experience less notable events as adults because when we're young, everything is new. But the truth is that we're the ones who have kept ourselves around the familiar in lieu of embracing a more youthful mindset and doing the work necessary to continue our evolution. It's up to us to find more experiences or add more to our timeline. If not, we risk becoming the cliché of the guy still telling the story of his home-run hit when he was nine years old.

Care to kick-start your own revolution? There are exercises at the back of the book and online, so you can't escape it. Like any forcible overthrowing of the status quo in favor of a new system, it takes a bit of strategy and some effort, but once you see the opportunity for a new outcome, the status quo is simply doomed.

See the exercises at the back of the book or visit SuccessHangover.com for more.

GOING SHOPPING

How do you go about getting new experiences? The key is to engage in experiences outside of your default. For example, Lollapalooza could be an incredible experience and place to stock ingredients. But I've been several times and none of my friends would be surprised to hear I went. I can still go and have an emotional engagement, but it will be stocking an eye-level ingredient and won't spice anything up. I may have trouble distinguishing it from other years I've gone—the memory will be hazy. What if I went to a death metal concert instead? I'd probably be scared out of my mind. Meanwhile, those at the concert would be saying, "What the hell is that mom doing here?" Now, when I tell my friends about the experience at the next dinner party, my story is suddenly interesting. My friends are craning their necks at the table to listen. It was unexpected, if not a tad hilarious. And finally, I'm sure to remember it and many nuances about and within it. Heck, I might even find inspiration, an aha connection there.

When you ask yourself, "What use will this ingredient give me in the future?" remember, no one knows, because we don't know the future. But you will certainly remember your new ingredient more than your eye-level, default ingredients. It's the difference between adding yet another bottle of oregano versus a bottle of red pepper flakes. Even if you don't cook spicy dishes, chances are there will come a time that spice will be of use.

UNINTENTIONAL OBSOLESCENCE IN OUR PERSONAL AND BUSINESS LIVES

The notion of becoming unintentionally obsolete happens both at work and in our personal lives. However, it may be more painful to feel obsolete on one side more than the other. Maybe it's more agonizing to feel obsolete in your personal life than in your business life. Whatever the case, it's natural to have unbalanced pain points. Because of that, it will be easier to make adaptations on one side as well. I'm more comfortable making adaptations in the business world because I've always taken risks there. For some, the business side will be more difficult. The reactions from those in your business life will surely differ from those in your personal life. Colleagues may take to your transformations as your play to steal their jobs, which postulates more reason to use baby steps. Spouses or friends may assume you're flirting with the mailman when they see you so reinvigorated. In any case, we must make adaptations on both sides because our personal and business lives work synergistically. Again, it's all about momentum. Who can deny that when his job's going well, that positivity spreads to his personal life and vice versa?

Some of the adaptations we make will affect both our personal and our business lives simultaneously. Recently, I dyed my hair red—a crazy red. I have been a fake blonde for years. When my husband, Andrew, came home, he was surprised (maybe a little shocked) by the red, but ultimately, he liked it. There was a chance he'd hate it, but what was the worst thing that could have happened? We weren't getting divorced over it. The reaction at work was different and based on functionality. Do we need to update our press materials? Do CEOs have red hair? I looked more the predictable part with streaked blond hair, but no one gave me less time of day with red hair.

If you haven't made many recent adaptations to yourself or your world, dying your hair a new color may bring on slightly greater risk. Start small. Remember, it's about baby steps, building momentum, and adapting every day. We all know midlife-crisis guy, right? He's the one who lived quietly until...bam! He woke up one day, bought a Corvette, dyed his hair, pierced his nipples, and started listening to hip-hop within a week. Futureproofing is not about going big, shooting fireworks. Fireworks have a finale, then dissipate.

By collecting new ingredients and making small adaptations every day, we get back in tune with our lives, and dissecting our pain points becomes easier. Maybe we've been blaming our troubles on our marriage when the pain point derived from the young hotshot who got the promotion we wanted. Maybe we're blaming our careers for boring us when it's we who have lost our edge.

Getting your edge back doesn't mean you're living on the edge; it means you're *alive*. You live rich as opposed to simply surviving. We want to talk to the people living this way. We want to be around them. We notice them come into the room. In the next chapter, we'll learn how to go from *noticing* that person to *being* that person.

MAYBE WE'RE BLAMING OUR CAREERS
FOR BORING US WHEN IT'S WE WHO
HAVE LOST OUR EDGE.   — KR

YourNextAct

Chapter 4

THE MOST INTERESTING PERSON IN THE ROOM

Why should you be the most interesting person in the room rather than the most successful? And how the hell does one become the most interesting person in the room anyway? First, realize that being successful and relevant correlate to being interesting, but it's the latter that has longevity. People are fascinated by what's new. Our minds are wired to seek information and will subconsciously identify extraordinary people. So what does that mean exactly? It means that if you're not interesting, you'll blend into the woodwork. You'll get passed over and plateau within status quo. Screw that.

The world tells us it wants something new, driven by our very desire for it. Whether it's twenty-four-hour news, the latest technology, or what neighbor Suzy Creamcheese just did, we can't get enough. Given we're predisposed this way, it's no wonder we notice someone across the room who appears different and emits a novel aura. We are not genetically wired to notice the person who outworked everyone else. We'll never weave the crowd to get a glimpse of that elusive workhorse who peed less and did more. If we were, we'd notice most MBA grads, lawyers, and doctors who walked into a room. On the other end of the spectrum, while we're sure to notice flashy people wearing sequins and flashing jazz hands (the equivalent of a loud, brusque, and somewhat desperate person), our BS meter will go off and down simmers any interest.

Here's the key: you only need to be the most interesting person in the room that matters to you. If you're an advertising person, you don't need to be the most interesting person in an engineer's room. It's an impossible feat to be the most interesting person in every room. Focus on those relevant to you.

HOW THE HELL DO I BECOME THE MOST INTERESTING PERSON IN THE ROOM?

I used to think there was something weird about me. I spent much of my life wondering if there was food on my face, because everyone always noticed me. Even today, whenever I'm at a red light, I'll snake eye to the next car to confirm the other person is guaranteed to be looking at me. I don't stand out in any extreme way, so why?

The most interesting people in the room are those who are most alive; they are magnetic. Not those who just breathe and exist but those who maximize their lives and take each day as a chance to improve. Anyone can do it. You don't need to be an extrovert or a showman; in fact, you don't even need to open your mouth to exude magnetism (which may be good news if you're an introvert). Nor must you be the most beautiful, funniest, or loudest person in the room. Magnetic people stick out because they don't abide by the status quo; they're the folks walking to the beat of their own drums—and they've got a killer beat. I always identify these people immediately because I know they have interesting things to say, and not only will I learn something from them, but they also save me from having to hold the dinner party conversation by myself. Again, don't forget this person applies to *my* interests and makes sense in my world, perhaps not directly at first but always somehow in the end. I'm not at a dinner party for neonatal surgeons and won't notice the same person surgeons will. I only notice and aim to be the most interesting person in a relevant room to my life.

Compare our hypothetical room to Instagram. I don't follow neonatal surgeons because their posts aren't relevant to me (truthfully, they'd freak me out). I want to follow people posting photos of art, music, and unique experiences because that's what I like. Most users within these categories, however, post images lacking variety and depth. How many selfies in front of landmarks are intriguing? My eyes stop on thought-provoking images—those that spark my curiosity and with commentaries that bring the human experience to life. What photo are you apt to spend more time on: the one of the girl in front of the Eiffel Tower (i.e., "Me in front of the #EiffelTower! #Selfie #BoxChecked #EveryoneDoesIt #Boring") versus the Eiffel Tower shot with half a profile and a commentary about the relationship between the United States and France, relating the Eiffel Tower to the Statue of Liberty and current economic times. I'd find the second post interesting and relevant even if Paris wasn't on my bucket list.

CONNECTIONS 2.0

Gone are the days when networking happened around a table of drinks. That's not to say these happy hours no longer exist, but the sexiness has faded. The old networking ways were based on your title, the logo on your card, and the people you had access to. It was surface level and terribly superficial. Bravo, you lowered your inhibitions at a mixer, swapped cards with a slew of people, then wondered what they could do for you—end of story. The business card said it all as little changed in one's career:

IBM Jill was probably still IBM Jill two years later, and sadly, we knew nothing else about her. We didn't know she's been to Spain several times or that she skateboards during the weekend.

Today's version of IBM Jill became Diply Jill after a year at IBM, moved from the States to Canada, and may no longer have a relevant network for me. Our circles of influence expanded incredibly. In the past, I may have done business with people within a hundred-mile radius and all of my contacts fit in a Rolodex. How big a Rolodex would you need to fit all your LinkedIn contacts into today? This network expansion resulted in the loss of true connections.

How many of your LinkedIn contacts have you shaken hands with? Imagine your 1,500 LinkedIn contacts stacked as business cards. How would anyone stand out? Cards are no longer there physically, and one's presence is essentially code in a cloud. Such is the new, modern world of networking, which is why we should consider a contact's potential trajectory. Sure, we note where she works (IBM Jill) and we still wonder who she has access to (IBM VPs?), but the real question to ask is, what will this person do next (create a new technological revolution)? Ask yourself if this person will do something relevant and interesting for your world, or you for his or hers.

GUILTY BY ASSOCIATION

Few people would have seen my Rolodex in the past, whereas today, everyone can see with whom I'm connected. Consequently, we put ourselves on the line, and our networks have become bloated and at times useless because of the 1,500 contacts—you probably truly trust only 200. Ask yourself what you know about a potential new connection aside from job title before signing on, because job titles are sure to change. We should make connections based on character, integrity, and direction. We should also consider passing prospective connections to friends who make a better match. Not all invitations are good. Protect your social networks because there are plenty of ways to crack them.

If you see a politically charged post on my Facebook page, you may think differently of me, even if my friend wrote it. In the past, this type of guilt by association was more likely to occur if you brought "that guy"—a friend who drank too much and embarrassed you—to a networking mixer. Unlike embarrassing memories from a drunken night out, what's published online doesn't fade away from the internet.

So what? This applies to you because you are also a code of ones and zeros in a cloud in someone else's connections on LinkedIn. What makes you exceptional and less of a risk?

Despite someone's great title and killer contacts, is connecting with him or her a risk? Is he or she *that* guy? Will he add genuine value to you? Be sure someone is adding value before connecting. Connections should be based on quality over quantity. As they say, your network is your net worth, especially once you've run out of hoops to jump.

THE MISSING LINK

When you want to meet the president of a company, you don't need to go to the front door and ask his or her assistant for a meeting. Today, you crack the code by finding his/her email and leapfrogging the old gate-keeping system. Accordingly, people rise to the top from seemingly nowhere and "get in" while we're left wondering how they got there so fast. Our hypothetical person moved up because she developed meaningful relationships with important individuals within the company. And in the big sea of connections, we turn to those we trust and with whom we have a human connection.

If you're not the first person to come to mind because you're not that interesting, and if you're not around enough to feel trustworthy in the room that matters to you, someone else will be.

Take the time to make deep connections and get to know

the people in your network. Actively stock fresh, interesting ingredients. The more interesting you are, the less work you'll have forging meaningful connections because people will flock to you.

Did I mention this applies to your personal life as much as your professional life? No? Well, you are a bright bulb, so you already knew that and I'd hate to bore you with the obvious.

SURPRISE AND DELIGHT

Clean your network by first defining what interests you, then sifting through your contacts and asking yourself, *Is this person doing something interesting?* Resist the urge to rank people by title or think only CEO-level people are valuable. If you don't, you're sure to lose plenty of connections that will end up doing something interesting.

Do you remember everyone you've connected with? Do they remember you? Reach out and test the connection. Send a few emails to see what you get back. If someone can't take a few seconds to respond, do you need to be connected? Did this person only connect in hopes of leapfrogging you to get to someone else? Create a rank of hierarchy to see who matters. Send physical cards in the mail, schedule dinners, and reconnect in person for real conversations. It's phenomenal how people will respond when you take the time to reach out in a meaningful way. Few people do it, so you'll naturally stand out, raise your value, and become the intriguing person everyone's interested in. This is an opportunity to stop and stock ripe and ready-for-picking, at-your-fingertips ingredients **today**. Naturally, when done correctly, it fulfills all 3Es.

I like to photocopy pictures of myself with old colleagues and university buddies and send the images with quick notes such as, *We took this picture twenty-three years ago! I hope to send you an updated similar photo again twenty-three years from now!* We're all skeptical and expect others to reach out when they want something from us, whether a recommendation, introduction, or advice. You'll stand out that much more when your recipient learns you have no ulterior motive.

It's easy to say you don't have time for this challenge, but you do. Send a few letters a week and one invitation a month. Frankly, if you don't have thirty minutes a month to have coffee with someone, you've allowed yourself to think you're more important than you really are. Remember, it's all about building momentum with baby steps. If you set out to clean your networking group and connect with dozens of people by the end of the month, you'll either fail to get it done or do a poor job at the practice.

The practice of reaching out to your contacts only needs

to take forty-five minutes of your day every few weeks. It's one great practice that leads to another. Start taking the step—build yourself some damn momentum, otherwise what? Yep. You're stagnating.

IT'S ALL YOUR FAULT I SCREEN MY PHONE CALLS

Networking used to be a spiderweb designed to catch as many people as possible. It's an outdated concept, and worse, it misses the point. What help or inspiration will your connections provide if they don't know you or what your goals are? Once upon a time, we got lost in the fervent search for bigger and better and sought contacts in a box-checking manner. It's time to bring it back to the handshake enterprise era.

When you work with people who know you, they'll most likely treat you better. How much more difficult would it be to cancel a contract with someone you know and respect compared to a stranger? You'll put care into the work you do with trusted colleagues, and you'll be less likely to send nasty quick-reaction emails. Stakes are higher when you know the people you're doing business with, because there's nowhere to hide if you don't up your game.

The old networking spiderweb got so big that manners were lost and people became numbers. Take the time to get to know and (hopefully) trust those you work with and want to collaborate with in the future.

SOMEWHERE IN THE PARK

Stocking ingredients is what keeps us alive and interesting. In the corporate world, we frequently find ourselves at the same table with the same people having the same conversations. It's like old friends hashing out the same stories every time they reunite. The stories may be funny, but are they still interesting? They may be entertaining, but I'd rather be the most interesting person in the room than the most entertaining. New ingredients break these easy-to-fall-into patterns by freshening the perspective even in regurgitated conversations.

When you're continuously stocking new ingredients, you'll bring innovative solutions to the weekly standing meeting (let's say it's about product mix). The night before, you pushed outside your boundaries and went to the Latin District night market and saw an interesting texture that might work for your product. Then, when you put the idea out at the meeting, you change a static conversation.

We put far too much pressure on ourselves to dazzle at every table (whether the boardroom or dinner table) that we psyche ourselves out and decide to hide in our safe old mindsets. You don't have to hit home runs every day; an assist is just as productive. Think about introducing two people to bridge an interesting connection, that's an assist, and people love the assister. "Have you met Simon? I met him at the Latin District's night market, and he's a writer just like you."

Not every idea you have will be the solution, but it may be a step toward one the same way an assist is to a hockey goal. Stop thinking you need to know all the ingredients necessary for success. We don't have crystal balls, and we don't have the answers. We simply need to start gathering ingredients, mixing, testing, and trying.

ARE YOU LOOKING FOR HEALTHY CANDY?

Instead of watching CNN like you do every night, what if you invite eight people over to drink wine and discuss a business idea? Will you get new ingredients by inviting the eight friends you're most frequently with? Maybe, but odds are, you'll get the same responses you always do, and friends tend to tell you what you want to hear. The evening would count as a baby step in the right direction, but don't fool yourself disguising old ingredients as if they're new. It's like going to Whole Foods to be healthier and coming out with a candy bar. The Whole Foods bag doesn't mean it's any different.

The way you communicate your ingredient-stocking experiences is a great litmus test for their efficacy. What kind of story would you tell about the evening drinking wine and discussing a business idea with good friends? How would you feel and what emotion would you convey? What would the reactions be? Bored, indifferent? What if you invited eight people outside your default circle, all with different careers and backgrounds instead? How would the conversation change? How would the way you relay the story change? You'd naturally communicate the latter with more intrigue and interest. You'd be more alive telling the story because it was outside your defaulted norm, and therefore you can't help but light up when you discuss it.

You'll feel the difference when you expand your ingredient-collecting further outside your norms, and you'll communicate the experiences differently, too. You'll emit natural enthusiasm and become the storyteller that people want to listen to.

It's simple: stock new ingredients outside your norm, and you'll have an interesting story to tell and a new recipe card to index and adapt from.

THE KEY TO THE COOL CLUB

What have your usual ingredients done for you lately? I

religiously read the *Economist* because it helps me stay abreast with relevant stories, and I can hold a conversation on a long list of topics. But it's not often I read a story so interesting that I'm tempted to rip the page out and keep it. Ultimately, the *Economist* works well but so do my closest friends. There's no need for me to eliminate them. But if I'm stocking my go-to safe supply ingredients only, will they do anything for me?

Futureproofers are in the party we all secretly want to be invited to but make excuses why we're not. We notice futureproofers, we may even spite them, but ultimately, we want to be in their club. Rest assured there's no secret key or hidden door to the party. Futureproofers live rich because they're constantly feeding themselves new ingredients. They're not bragging; they're not atrocious. They're just more alive because they're more active. They don't live their lives on default.

Futureproofers are more interesting but not more important. It's crucial to remember the difference. When I ride home from a dinner party in my minivan (and yes, with three kids, I drive a minivan), I'll want to talk about the most interesting person I met, not the top of the party's social hierarchy (though every so often it's the same person).

When you step out of your routine and collect new

ingredients, they'll work for you in ways you cannot yet predict. You'll feel the difference, and you'll get into that damn club.

THE TANTRIC GARDENER

Futureproofing is not an extreme sport. You don't need to wake up and drink your morning coffee upside down in Dubai (although that would be an interesting story to tell). Futureproofing does not mean you completely leave behind your normal routines either; you still need to keep the garden tidy. There will always be boxes to check, but you can check them in new ways. We talked earlier about getting stuck in the missionary sex of your career, but let's be honest, missionary sex still counts. Missionary sex is better than nothing, but eventually, it will become background noise and not very memorable.

Take baby steps outside your missionary position, collect easy ingredients, and over time, you'll expand your shelves to new heights. Your garden will be tidy *and* sexy.

ARE YOU THAT PERSON?

We view the world in a very scientific way. We measure people with quantifiable terms such as grades, degrees, or how many countries they've visited, whereas we should view the world and its people with artistic interpretation.

If you go to the MoMA and observe a big white canvas, what will you think? Most people dismiss the work as child's play and worthless. Many will label it ridiculous, too afraid to consider it more deeply and to find reason and meaning where it isn't clear in an obvious or traditional way. One's quick rejection stems from not wanting to be viewed silly, crazy, or "out there" by daring to profess a subjective opinion.

The white canvas artist most certainly had a meaning in addition to guts and courage. But sadly, as a society, we've been led in the opposite direction of innovation. That's why we're apt to minimize work we don't understand, or keep quiet when we feel we don't know enough to make an educated comment. We've been focusing on the clouds in the sky instead of noticing their shape or— next-level stuff—the shapes of the glorious blue behind them (the way we did as a child). When you play it safe and stick to your default reaction, you miss stocking a new ingredient. You can be physically present at the museum, but if you don't check in and ask yourself what you see and how it makes you feel, there's no point. The same goes for a day in the office.

We can't keep thinking we already know everything. We don't. And the faster we admit that and become curious again, the more open to new experiences we'll be, and we'll stock richer ingredients.

We all have an operating system in our set of rules. We've allowed these rules to define who we are and what we do. But consider this: becoming exceptional requires making an exception to the rule. I ask every client I work with if he wants to be exceptional with everything he does, and the answer is always yes. But that's an impossible task if you're operating by the same set of rules and putting the same cards down at every game.

WHAT YOUR RULES SAY ABOUT YOU

Our immediate reactions stem from our set of rules. I have a friend who can't make up her mind about anything, so I flip a coin to push her. Heads means our usual bar; tails means we go across town to a seedy bingo hall. When seedy bingo hall wins and she frets, her reaction shows it's contrary to her set of rules. How do her rules apply in said scenario? She doesn't feel she belongs on this side of town? She's uncomfortable having others judge her for being wealthier than them? She doesn't play bingo? It could be any one (or all) of these things. What's important to recognize is how they're keeping her in her default.

Our set of rules may be so deeply rooted that we can't pinpoint when or why we developed them. Without going into psychoanalysis, what we can do is become aware of the reactions we're making and question them. Whenever you immediately dismiss something, stop and address the situation: why are you against it? Push outside your set of rules and baby step your way out. It can be as simple as working in the candlelight if you always work with the lights on. It's that easy. Whenever you challenge your set of rules and break from your default, the experience will be more memorable. The practice will activate you into the present and make you more alive. It also gives you a shot at strategically stocking your mental shelves instead of spending another minute working hard only to have all your effort end up as the spilled flour on the floor, sure to be swept up and discarded. Your hard work should be applied to your next culinary masterpiece, not wasted.

Remember to ask again what your rules are doing for you. Then start by choosing one to make an exception for. Think of one of your idols: what did he do that was exceptional? Oprah didn't get a lucky strike; she observed what was happening in her space and did the opposite. She's a leader because she had the guts to remove the cards in her deck that kept her playing safe.

Anytime you apply an exception to your rule, you become exceptional. The more you do it, the more exceptional you'll be.

YOU'RE GOING TO HATE ME

Corporations are desperate to be innovative and cutting

edge, yet most have endless sets of rules. But what is an organization at the end of the day? Nothing more than a summation of humans. Those in charge can either use rules to whip others into shape or spur their teams to show up with ideas. Futureproofers help corporations become exceptional when they make exceptions to the rules.

When I work with organizations, I request the attendees to come from various departments so everyone isn't totally familiar with one another. I ask everyone to introduce him-/herself without saying where s/he is from, what s/he does, if s/he's married, or has children. How quickly the process of elimination renders the group uncomfortable! They suddenly hate me. Despite how educated, smart, and successful the attendees may be, they're now unsure what to say. How sad, right? Because the question is targeted to the core of who they are.

It's not our fault. Social conditioning teaches us to wear masks that we tighten so much over time that we forget who's underneath. That's why we're stuck when asked to introduce ourselves without using traditional tags. The other reason we get stuck is because we haven't done anything interesting recently. If you haven't stocked any ingredients as of late, nothing comes to mind. All the participants may be there physically and can raise their hand to say, "Present!" just as they did when schoolteachers did roll call. But they've been taught to stop there.

By asking people to introduce themselves without easy labels, we take away their boxes to check. Yet it's the stripping of boxes that makes a person and his or her unique ingredients interesting and memorable.

To push the group further, I'll write a list of accomplishments I assume most share, such as an MBA or a degree, and ask everyone to physically check the boxes next to the items. I then draw a line across the board on top of all those boxes to show the level everyone collectively reached. In other words, everyone is equal until that point, and therefore talking about anything within the collectively shared boxes would be like saying, "Hi, my name is Kelsey, and I know my ABCs." Gee, how interesting is Kelsey?

Sharing assumed information is boring.

Go on, introduce yourself. Nothing assumed will do now.

Daunting as it may be to refine who you say you are to others, what about a reintroduction to who you are when you are alone? Try it. Then reintroduce yourself as you are, everywhere you go and with anyone you meet. See if it makes you feel alive again.

Hello, you. I'll meet you at the back of the book where you'll do the exercise titled: Introduce Yourself.

RISKY BUSINESS

Although Mr. Tolstoy is correct about change, and we all love an immediate rebirth, futureproofing is about evolving through adaptation, not change. Change is drastic. Change is moving from one city to another, or at its most basic level, it's changing the sheets. Change in physical terms sticks far easier than it does for humans. In other words, it's easier to change the state of water by putting it on the burner to boil than it is to get a person to change and start going to the gym regularly.

Let's be bold and adapt Tolstoy's quote, "An absolute lack of *adaptation* means death in the mental as well as the physical world."

We don't need to transform from monkey to human, so let's not talk ourselves out of it. Futureproofing is not about making a wholesale shift; it's about adapting. Adaptation is a nuance of change. Instead of moving to Cincinnati tomorrow, you could take the train there this weekend and check it out first.

People tend to panic when their company makes a lot of changes, but if they'd been adapting all along, it wouldn't be so drastic. Anything feels less risky when you approach it as a daily adaptation rather than a big change.

Adaptation happens over time with bits and pieces.

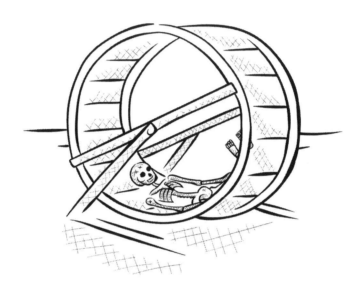

AN ABSOLUTE LACK OF
ADAPTATION MEANS DEATH
IN THE MENTAL AS WELL
AS THE PHYSICAL WORLD.

#YourNextAct

We shouldn't wait for change like Chicken Little any more than we should cling to false hope and assume our world will revolutionize on January 1 (or even the coming Monday).

We want our lives to get better quickly, but abrupt changes don't stick. Futureproofers make daily adaptations to avoid unintentional obsolescence, to become alive again, and pursue act two—success 2.0.

WHY IT'S NEVER TOO LATE TO WIN

Resistance to adaptation takes on many forms. I often hear the excuse, "I got left behind, and it's too late to catch up." Imagine a starting line on a track with seven racers lined up. The race begins, but guess what? Three of them inexplicably leave the race, and two others barely move. As for the one who looks like she's going to win? Suddenly, she trips. The point is, we don't know the future and we don't know who will win. There is never a reason to feel too far behind to quit the race.

Simply walking the racecourse is good, but if you're trying to become exceptional and get ahead, being good is akin to being mediocre. Consistency alone is the new glass ceiling, and you won't break through being good all the time. Yes, you can get through life being good, but you'll quickly become the vanilla cake of your career and personal life. You'll be viewed as reliable and comfortable despite feeling you've got more to offer. If that's the case, it's insane to keep stocking vanilla and nothing else.

Remember, keep adapting from your default. You need diverse, fresh ingredients to stay in the race.

NEXT STOP: YOUR DEFAULT FUTURE

When you don't make adaptations in your life, you become the ostrich lifting his head from time to time to see what's coming but ultimately going back down for a graze. If what's coming is your company about to downsize, and if all you bother to do is lift your head enough to complain about the incoming change, you waste time creating anxiety instead of preparing for the inevitability. You're the one who's good and consistent, but you were never exceptional. Even now, you're just standing there waiting for things to happen instead of acting.

What will happen if you're not willing to prepare for what's next and develop the capacity to adapt? The answer is your default future. The downsizing company is not looking for good people; it's looking for adaptable people who can handle something new. In the great scheme of the cosmos, it's the adapters who survive. Ask Charles.

Your default future is coming. Make a choice while you

have the chance. Move away from "What if something happens?" to "How are we going to *make* something happen?"

QUADRANT EXERCISE

I created this little beauty of a strategic model to help myself focus on where I spend my days.

It just might be the most powerful piece of work I've created for people like us.

I created it years ago and it continues to be my north star when I need clarity, focus and a no-BS view of where I'm showing up or hiding out. If you do just one exercise from this book, this is the one to do. Head to the back and look for The Quadrant Exercise now.

How you spend your days
is How you spend your life.
                    —Annie Dillard.

Your Next Act

Book Three

ADAPT TO IT

Chapter 5

THE INGREDIENTS

Where do you start collecting new ingredients? How should they differ from those you already have? Because you have a lot of ingredients, it's likely you're not using them all effectively. Regardless of how many you have, it's essential to continuously seek more. If you don't, you stop evolving, and soon, you'll have nothing to differentiate yourself and move you forward. You'll stagnate.

It's easy to keep restocking the same ingredients because it's safe. When you love pad thai, you order it every time it's on the menu. Before long, you're surrounded by other people who love pad thai and your world narrows. Is that how you want to feed your mind?

Maybe you love languages and you're involved in Spanish-speaking groups and have plenty of Spanish-speaking friends. You stick with Spanish because you're good at it—it's safe. What if you adapted your language skills to try a French or Chinese class? Now, you're still in your realm of interest, but you're stocking totally new ingredients—that is to say, tools, skills, experiences, and people.

SUPERMARKET SWEEP

Picture a supersized all-purpose store like Costco. The second you walk in, you feel dwarfed; the place is the size of a football field, maybe bigger. There are gigantic aisles everywhere, all of them filled. The store has absolutely everything you can imagine, all in bulk, and at a relatively low cost; it can be overwhelming. It's totally feasible that at some point while shopping, you forget what you came to find and won't know how the hell to get out. What does this monolith market compare to in terms of information sources? If you guessed the media, you guessed right. Let's think of Costco as the media (the internet of news and information). You got that? Shopping at Costco is our media consumption.

Now picture a convenience store. It's stocked with quick and delicious options: cookies and chips, stuff that tastes great but none of it is nutritious. This is social media. It's like gossip, a quick hit that keeps you wanting more but never truly satiates (and the more time you spend catching up on everyone else's lives, the less you spend on your own). So again, think of this convenience store as social media.

Finally, imagine a local organic market, one you go to for the lemongrass in your pad thai recipe. While there, you get into a conversation with the purveyor about other delicious uses for lemongrass, and he tells you a great recipe for tom yum soup. You come out of the specialized market with something aside from what was on your list, and it's purposeful, has you excited, and later you tell your partner about your experience as you dine on the tom yum soup you made along with the pad thai. This local, specialized shop doesn't always have what you went to get, but it often surprises you with something you don't know much about.

Which of these three stores (Costco, the convenience mart, or the local shop) do you want to stock most of your ingredients? Now ask yourself this: where have you been doing most of your shopping? And where do you need to *start* shopping to gain diverse ingredients? Make a list of your usual routine and then consider the roles your hypothetical stores play in stocking your shelves. What is your brain consuming the most? Do you have enough ingredients to support what you take out, or are you running low (i.e., do you really need to stock more photos of cute puppies from Facebook)?

Have you ever had to write down everything you ate for

a time? Even if you haven't, imagine doing it. Imagine writing down every little thing you put in your mouth. It can be a surprising practice, especially if it's going to be analyzed by someone else. After a day or two of seeing everything you ate all written out, you may feel inspired to eat better foods. You may feel embarrassed to show your doctor (or even yourself) that you're surviving on coffee and cookies. Or that you eat a pack of cookies in the afternoon. Now imagine you had to list your ingredient-stocking markets for others to see. That includes your friends and colleagues. Would they be surprised to learn how many hours you spend in Costco (i.e., consuming media)? How about the total sum of time spent in your convenience store (aka liking things on Facebook)? Wouldn't we prefer to show we spend most of our time in interesting, specialized markets?

Now imagine feeding your Costco or convenience store program to your children or children you care for. Would you want them spending that much time with the media or that many hours on Twitter? We don't feed our kids crap, so why do we do it to ourselves?

What are you feeding that hungry mind?

Take stock with the exercise called What Are You Feeding Your Mind.

We must continuously stock interesting ingredients to spur aha moments. The ingredients help us grow; you can't expect to get adequate nutrients by eating plain white noodles all the time. The more ingredients you have in your fridge, the more diverse dishes you'll make. *Ah yes, I have cilantro. We can do tacos tonight.* When you stock more ingredients, you look at the world differently because you're meeting new people and endlessly expanding your horizons. You're talking to the shop purveyor and learning a new recipe instead of waiting robotically in a long line at Costco.

WHEN INSIGHTS ARE THE ENEMY

Are you ready to start stocking new ingredients? Once you start, you'll build momentum and never want to stop. If you don't start, you'll stagnate; then you'll end up in your default future.

There's a natural tendency to want to get hyper strategic involving our search for ingredients. While some strategy is helpful, too much will turn the practice into a box-checking process. Remember, we don't know the future, so we don't know which ingredients we'll need, how they'll serve us, and when. We must constantly stock an array of options for that precise reason: the unknown future.

Companies work the same way in that they rely on insights to predict the future. Insights allow them to have a scapegoat when things go awry. Insights are playing it safe (like the top left side of the quadrant from the last chapter's exercise). If you're old enough to remember Beta (as in Betamax, the videotape format pre-VHS), then you know how they fell into this trap. Beta dominated the market share and gained many early adapters from whom they got their insights. Then the VHS format came along and stole the market with better marketing and increased partnerships. It didn't matter Beta's technology was better, because VHS offered diversity and that excited a larger group. Beta stagnated because they listened to only the early adapters and didn't adapt themselves to attract a larger audience.

If Henry Ford had relied on insights, he'd have given people a faster buggy instead of the car. Instead, he innovated what we didn't know was possible—and changed the world.

HUMBLE PIE

The first steps toward futureproofing are to do something unexpected. You can start by driving an unusual way to work, jogging a new route, ordering a dish you've never tried, or even changing your morning routine from setting your clothes out the night before to choosing them after your morning coffee. These are low-risk challenges, but they are the first and very necessary baby steps toward futureproofing and moving away from your default. By slowly breaking your routine, you're training to be nimble.

Doing something different can bring moments of discomfort. For example, if your strategy is to discuss something (let's say Japanese trade) with an expert, you may feel nervous because you're accustomed to being the authority and fear appearing uneducated. Futureproofing means putting yourself out there, humbling yourself enough to ask so-called dumb questions. Put yourself in a vulnerable position and you're more likely to learn something new. Odds are that the person you are speaking to will be able to tell you are not an expert either way. So let's not demean ourselves by pretending. Rather, let's elevate us both—your understanding and his or her value in expertise.

Don't forget you still have intuition. Intuition isn't the wanderlust concept of blindly going where the path takes you. Intuition is the culmination of your experiences: scholastic, emotional, and visceral; it's the sum of all your knowledge. When your gut tells you something, it's because your experiences are screaming through the noise to say, "I know this! Please value me over that damn paper hanging on your wall!" Take an active role listening to your intuition and then test your boundaries.

As a speaker around the world, I'm frequently put in a room full of experts on topics I may know very little about. Instead of getting intimidated, I admit when I'm asking an ignorant question. Those in the audience may think, *Geez, she doesn't know that? I thought she was this magical business genius who wins all these awards.* So be it. By asking questions, I learn something new; I'm active and alive as opposed to just being present and nodding my head. It brings us back to the Step Function Model: when you hit a plateau, will you stay there, or will you build another step?

We must familiarize ourselves with the emotions that come with being on the ledge, or we'll become the person who waits for the new step to appear—and we're back to stagnating. It's OK to feel, I promise.

THIS IS YOUR BRAIN ON...

When we do something repeatedly, our brains create strong neural pathways for the activity. Brains are muscles, and the more you travel a certain pathway, the more likely you'll continue to take that route. In other words, when our brain easily predicts what's about to happen and can easily travel the route needed to get the job done, it doesn't fully activate (cue the glazed-eyed look from people in weekly meetings).

We must stimulate our brains or they'll function like

involuntary muscles. It's standing order for your heart to beat and lungs to breathe. If we live our lives like standing orders, we stop being present. Yet we're shocked that we're so bored at work and that nothing new ever happens. What else could we expect when we allow ourselves to function so minimally? As James Allen said in *As a Man Thinketh*, "Let a man radically alter his thoughts, and he will be astonished at the rapid transformation it will effect in the material conditions of his life."

Life will become highway hypnosis if you let it. You'll reach a destination without remembering anything about the journey. Suddenly, you're asking yourself, "How the hell did I get passed by for that promotion?" You got passed because you never did anything exceptional, and while you were simply being present, Johnny Come Lately came up with a kick-ass idea.

GO, ESCARGOTS!

Imagine three snails racing on skateboards—just do it. The snail in first place is stretched out, his antennae reaching forward. The snail in second place is close behind and intently focused on the snail in first place. The third-place snail is on the track but so unfocused that a bird could come down and snatch him at any moment, bite right onto the juicy part between his shell and head, and poof! He's toast. All he did was show up. He's doing the minimum of what we expect of a snail on a skateboard (because there are so many snails on skateboards, of course).

Meanwhile, the second-place snail is so focused on the first-place snail that he requires him to be there—ahead of him. We all do this at some point, yet we expect to win. By waiting for the prescription of what to do next, you'll always be behind. It's not our fault; we were taught to wait for instructions. But the truth is, we've been lied to.

The snail in first place is doing what we were taught *not* to do, which is to stick his neck out. A bird could kill him, too! Yet it's that risk that got him to first place—not that he'll tell anybody else his secret. But he'll have to keep adapting his moves, because there will always be someone watching and studying the first-place snail. If he doesn't adapt, the second-place snail might catch onto his moves and tie. And doesn't it feel like shit to tie after all that work? It's almost better to lose, because then you have a goal again.

The finish line will always move forward. After Roger Bannister became (in 1954) the first runner in history to break the four-minute mile, hordes of men trained to do the same thing and did it in short order, making Bannister's accomplishment the new standard. The same applies to business. If you focus on beating someone else's accom-

plishment, you'll remain in the pack. It's vital to stock your shelves with new ingredients so you're capable of breaking the standard, being an exception to your rule, and ultimately to becoming exceptional.

Tune into your life, get behind the wheel, and break out of your default. Otherwise, you risk living a life of highway hypnosis and getting to the end without remembering how you got there.

_____ LIVED A _____ LIFE.

#YourNextAct

Chapter 6

———

EMBEDDED EXPERIENCES

How do you pick and choose the types of ingredients that will instigate solutions and lift you into exceptionalism? First, we need to be open to collecting the ingredients. As adults, we've turned into annoying defensive drivers waiting for someone to come into our lane to justify being pissed off. We're so worried about getting to our destination that we reject what's around us. But guess what? There are ingredients ripe for the picking everywhere.

Our ingredients shouldn't be stones we're randomly collecting but the result of one part strategy meets three parts nimbleness. Sadly, the further we go through life, the less active we become curating new ingredients. We wait for them to haphazardly arrive like an invitation or that jerky driver in our lane. It's easy to push aside the idea of procuring more experiences (they'll take up more of our already precious time!). The problem is, we end up burning said time bragging about how busy we are as if it's a contest in which we're excelling. Worse, we reject new experiences in claiming we're booked. Booked doing what? Working late and taking the kids to soccer? Great, everyone else is doing that, too. This closed mindset transforms our lives into agendas, and we get stuck collecting the same ingredients, shopping in the same stores, and making the same moves.

While ingredients are everywhere, we must engage some strategy in our procurement—just not so much we predefine the experiences and devoid their value. For example, if you plan a weekend rock-climbing trip (which falls outside your defaulted norm) but proceed to spend the whole week surmising how it will go, how you will feel during the experience, and what it will give you in the future, you're back to checking boxes. It's like doing an Easter egg hunt with a map.

We have to approach experiences with an open mind and remain curious. Stay flexible enough to change your path.

ONCE UPON A TIME, SOMETHING HAPPENED, THE END

While we shouldn't spend time predetermining how we'll feel before an experience, it's essential to ask plenty of questions during it. My daughter recently had to write about a personal connection she made between her life and an assigned school reading. She didn't get very far when she came to me for help. She had only two lines comparing the protagonist's dead pet to her dead fish. Dead pet, dead end, now what? I asked her questions: how did you feel when your fish died? How did the character feel? Did your fish have a name? Would you feel differently if your dog died instead of the fish? How would you memorialize your dog versus your fish?

When we question nothing, we're left with very little, and we stop learning. We only stock ingredients by staying curious, observant, and treating everything as if we may be interrogated about it later.

I NOW CALL TO THE STAND...

If you were called to the witness stand on any given day, how much would you recall? Would you be a reliable witness? Do you remember the conversations you had, what people were wearing, how you felt at any given moment, and what was happening in the background?

A good witness notices details. He observes what's happening. His emotion may be involved, however—and this is key—he doesn't judge and categorize the information at the outset. It's the difference between saying, "The man was wearing a blue shirt, and I felt scared," and, "The man was wearing a blue shirt, and he looked super shady."

The second you judge what you see, you stop seeing it for what it is. If you aren't witnessing, it's because your ego got involved and wants only to process the information as it relates to *you*. I'm sorry to tell you this, but the world does not revolve around you, so you'd better start witnessing what's actually happening.

When you approach life from a witnessing position, you observe your responses and environment, and you start to question. What's that person doing here? Has she been here before? How does that relate to the environment?

Think about a picky eater—maybe it's a toddler (maybe it's you). A picky eater judges and dismisses new dishes before he's tried them. He wants to eat chicken fingers because they're safe. *Chicken curry? No, I don't like that— that's yucky!* Sadly, if he does try it, he'll have already convinced himself he doesn't like it, to the point that he doesn't truly taste the dish and the experience voids itself.

It sounds like a riddle, but take a moment to reflect on the difference between observing your feelings versus judging your observations. You can observe anger. The judgment of the feeling is negative. What if you witness pain but you don't categorize it as bad? Overpower your desire to judge and rise above the pain you've always judged as a bad thing. It takes training, but over time, you can relearn how to experience a feeling without judging—and that's crucial so that you're not judging yourself. You may feel like an idiot at times, but what if you looked at that as a positive trait?

Discerning between observing your feeling without judging your observations is crucial so you don't ruin an experience by questioning your worth. Again, leave your damn ego at the door. Wherever you are and whatever you're doing, stop worrying about how you're being perceived. If you're thinking about yourself, you compromise the experience, your surroundings fade, and you lose the experience for what it's worth. Then when asked about it, all you'll be able to remember is how awkward you felt; you won't be able to explain what happened. When I walk into a room, I imagine those before me seeing me the same way I see them—the good old golden rule. When I need to ramp that up, I tell myself I give zero fucks. It's amazing how a little inner pep talk can take you out of your ego. Plus, whenever you appear to give zero fucks about how others perceive you, you naturally emit a cooler aura.

Removing your judgment from your experiences doesn't happen overnight. Stop and take a moment to ask yourself what you're witnessing; remove your judgment and just experience. Like everything, the more often you do this, the more natural it will become.

Suspend judgment for a moment and witness for yourself.

It'll take only a few minutes to see anew after you complete the section called Questions for Witnessing. You can also print it out for a good time at SuccessHangover. com.

TIME FOR A MAGIC TRICK: THE 3E METHOD IN PRACTICE

Let's do an experiment, shall we? I'm going to ask you two questions. Simply answer them and then continue reading.

Question: Think of something you know very well.

Got it?

Great.

Now think of something you remember, a memory.

Got it?

Good.

Here's where I read your mind. That thing you "know," the answer to the first question, I'll bet it can be taught. Could you teach it to someone? Or look it up in a book or Google it?

I'll bet the answer is yes.

And that memory, the thing you remember? I'm willing to bet it has three components to it:

- There is/was emotion involved (love, hate, fear, joy, etc.).
- Whatever it is/was, it could not be repeated. It could not be repeated the same way twice.
- Either you shared the experience with another human while it happened, or afterward, you shared it through communication to someone in person (not digitally).

Am I right?

Mind blown?

Now the crux, where you begin to love or hate me. Can we agree that if something can be taught, I can conceivably be programmed?

Try this test out on your friends; it works every time. Now that you *know* this trick, you can be the magician.

Why does this matter? Well, because it has the power to shift your parade, shift you into act two. But there's bad news: that little thing you *know* isn't that special. Anyone can learn it, and we can teach it to a robot. With that addressed, I do not want to discredit training. Yes, you still need training, but remember, it's an equalizer. Everyone can get training, and if you don't expand beyond yours, you'll be on the same wavelength as everyone else who did the same training. How do you become exceptional? That comes with what you remembered from our game. That's the special stuff, that's a real commodity because it cannot be replicated. It's what makes you *you*. It differentiates you more than anything you know, and it's where your real values lie.

THE STRATEGY TO EMBEDDING MEMORIES

What makes something memorable? When you go about your day, what will your brain vet and decide to stock as a useful ingredient for an unknown future day? Do you remember getting your regular morning coffee at Starbucks last year on March 14? Unless you have hyperesthesia, chances are extremely high you won't remember that day—unless something happened that elicited your emotions during the experience. Perhaps a man spilled his coffee all over your shirt, or the barista told you a joke that made you laugh until you snorted. To lift an experience out of ambiguity—and give your brain reason to store it indeterminably—the experience must elicit emotion.

THE 3E MODEL

1. **Experience**: engaging in experience
2. **Emotion**: an experience-related emotional response
3. **Embed**: communicating the experience with another human being

The first step is simply to have a **new experience**, which could not be repeated the same way twice. Earlier, we talked about the importance of an experience falling outside your defaulted norm. A new experience is obviously not going to your regular coffee shop, but it could be as simple as going to a coffee shop on the other side of town and ordering something you've never tried before.

The second vital step to strategically stocking ingredients is that your experience elicits an **emotional response**. If your new experience does not engage your emotions, you will not remember it in an accessible, meaningful way, and it will not become an ingredient on your shelf. It will be lost. Because ultimately, if there's no emotion, you're not really paying attention, as Mary Helen Immordino-Yang explains in *Emotions, Learning, and the Brain*.

> Another process that is related to the study of memory and emotion, and that is an important prerequisite, to the recruitment of a neural network is attention. The last decade marks theoretical and methodical advances in the study of attention and its relationship to the devel-

opment of academic skills (Corbetta & Shulman, 2002). In particular, Posner and his colleagues have distinguished three different attentional networks important for learning: networks for alerting, orienting, and executive attention.

After you've had a new experience that emotionally engaged you, the final step is to **embed it** by telling someone about it. The communication must be done traditionally, as in a good ol' tête-à-tête. Communicating via social media won't embed as a true engagement in your mind. As human beings, we crave telling someone else; it's part of our makeup as Mary Helen Immordino-Yang explains, this time in *Musings on the Neurobiological and Evolutionary Origins of Creativity*:

> What social and affective neuroscience studies are revealing is that the legacy of our intelligent brain is our social mind. By virtue of its evolutionary connection to bodily feeling and survival, our social mind motivates us to create things that represent the meaning we have made by process of noticing, feeling, and understanding, so that others can notice, feel, and understand what we have. While of course our bodies can no sooner live without food, water, and warmth than they ever could, these necessities alone are no longer sufficient for us. Our biological drives are co-opted over the course of cognitive development into a platform for making sense of the world in increasingly

complex ways. We must *understand,* we must *know,* we must *share our experiences.*

The communication component will result in one of two different ways: you'll either get affirmation or pushback. In other words, "Oh, that's cool!" or "Why did you do that?" The affirmation makes us feel good when people are excited or agree with what we've done or we tend to do more of. When someone pushes back, we may get defensive, lose motivation, and avoid further pursuits by deciding someone else's prerogative ranks higher. Recognize that these conversations may have an impact on your willingness to seek another experience. But remember that stopping means you're OK with your default future.

When you first start sharing your new experiences, it may be best to choose supportive people who may even want to join you in your pursuits. Later, when you're collecting ingredients like a ninja, you can share your experiences with naysayers (a rigid COO or your aunt Tilda who picks everything apart), while remaining confident enough in your futureproof lifestyle that their judgments don't dissuade you. Perhaps other people will be jealous or afraid of being left behind. I always question the bias behind the pushback before I put weight in it.

THE IMPORTANCE OF BEING EARNEST

Hearing yourself explain the experience is crucial. We express things differently depending on the medium we communicate in. Because we can easily backspace and move words around when writing on a computer, we may take more time writing on paper. When we speak, our thoughts come out in real time, and therefore, it's the truest relation of an experience because we can't contrive it in the same way we might were we to edit it later.

Our emotions are stronger when we verbalize them. Imagine the difference between admitting a loved one passed in your head versus telling someone else. Even if you planned how the conversation would go in your head, you're far more likely to get choked up when you say it aloud.

CREATING TECHNICOLOR MEMORIES

You need to tell only one person about your experience. But don't choose the person and the activity as if they're correlated or you're back to box-checking. Fulfilling an experience specifically to impress someone removes its authenticity. If you skydive to influence a skydive-loving boss, your story will likely be one of the many he's already heard. People love genuine, true, and emotionally charged stories.

An emotionally charged experience embeds in our minds

differently. Think of a photograph from your childhood. It may trigger a memory—"Ah yes, I was at Disney World"—but not necessarily the experience. If you had an emotional experience while at Disney because Goofy stole your hat and you cried, you'll recall it with far more clarity. Emotion brings a story to life and adds color to an otherwise colorless fact such as "I went to Disney World."

The further outside your default (safe gray world) that you stray, the more intense an experience's memory is likely to be. This doesn't mean you need to risk your life. You just need to put yourself far enough outside your routine to wake the hell up.

What's your morning routine look like? How can you change your morning routine a little bit? How can you change it a lot? Start with the *little bit*, and eventually, you'll crave the *a lot*.

DO YOU REMEMBER EVERY SINGLE FUCKING THING YOU KNOW?

There is a great quote by the Canadian band Tragically Hip: "I remember every single fucking thing I know." Sure, you may know everything you've read shortly after you've read it, but how much will you retain long term? Admit it, we forget an awful lot. When you no longer remember what you read or heard, you no longer know it.

To make it plain and simple: how much of what you studied do you know? Compare that to how much you know from putting lessons into practice through experience.

Stocking your shelves with memorable experiences raises your value. Consider having to choose between a heart surgeon who has read everything there is to know about heart surgery, or the doctor who read only a couple of books but performed actual surgeries dozens of times. The reason we call medicine a practice is because there's always more to learn. The same applies to you. Do you want to be the person who read every single book, or the one who did a lot of cool things?

We're talking about the practice of your life. Are you still practicing (i.e., are you still learning and expanding?), or did you already throw in the towel and retire?

LET'S TALK ABOUT STRATEGY, BABY

Let's look at five real people who strategized optimal futureproofing practices and built futureproofing steps in lieu of stagnating on the sad and lonely plateau.

SALLY HOGSHEAD

Sally Hogshead was running a highly successful multinational branding agency when the market turned, the economy collapsed, and her business took a major hit. With bills to pay, Sally found herself at the same crossroads countless others faced and had to decide her next move. She could sit on the sofa and check her boxes: this is my education, this is my experience, and this is the typical path for someone like me. Instead, she asked, "Who am I? What makes me unique?" Then she experimented within various fields to see what clicked.

Sally's strategy included interviewing thousands of people to learn what made them tick. In doing so, she realized people are truly their own brands. They create personas, styles, and strive to represent themselves in a certain fashion. She then connected her new recognition to her existing ability to improve brands and said, "I've been advising multinational brands how to earn more market share. What if I did that with individuals?"

Sally created the Fascination Advantage, a tool that defines an individual's unique brand, then helps him or her further understand and define what makes him or her interesting and marketable to the world. It hadn't been done before, so naturally, she met skepticism. "Sure, that's interesting, Sally, but what can you do with it?" What Sally did was turn it into a wildly successful, cutting-edge new business and became a *New York Times* best-selling author to boot.

Would Sally have innovated and given the world this

incredible gift had the market not tanked and her business been thriving? Who knows? The better question to ask is whether you have had the guts to be vulnerable and try something new when your business is either stagnating *or* thriving. Sally took her current knowledge, tapped into new experiences, and futureproofed her career.

JEN HANSARD

Jen Hansard was living a good life when the reality of mothering her second child took a toll on her energy. No amount of coffee perked her to the level she once knew. Balancing the roles of wife and mother and on little to no sleep, she was surviving, not thriving. Instead of accepting this fate, Jen expanded her environment and joined a mom group. There, she met someone out of her normal circle and learned about healthy green smoothies.

Jen got hooked on the smoothies, thanks to the pure energy she experienced. She began sharing this simple habit with friends and family, and the passion was contagious. In 2012, she partnered with a friend, the one who first introduced her to the green smoothies, and together they turned it into a business. They created an online community on Instagram and Facebook and shared their recipes. Within a year, they had two hundred thousand followers on Instagram. In the second year, they created an online plant-based program, Fresh Start, which became their main revenue generator. In 2015, they ended up generating nearly $1 million in revenue. In the last quarter of 2016, Jen bought her business partner out and pivoted again. She introduced a line of physical products to reinvigorate sales and turned her digital company into a physical brand.

Jen didn't set out to be a businessperson. But she was open, curious, and went after what made her happy. When that wasn't enough, she decided to share it with the world and now runs the wildly successful company Simple Green Smoothies. It's a great example of how staying curious sparks aha moments we'd never generate while stagnating at our desk.

CHRIS ANDERSEN

Chris Andersen was a chairman at Paine Webber, and as investment bankers do, he led a big life. Made tons of money. Sounds great, right? But this is a guy quoted for saying he gets off on challenges, so where does he go if he's already at the top on Wall Street?

Foodie that he is, he was out to eat at some fancy joint one night when he tried Mangalica pork. It was so damn good, he told *Forbes*, "It rocked me back to my socks." Great, he found something he loved. He could just keep eating it, right? No, it wasn't enough. Instead, he went to Spain to learn more about the Mangalica pig, and it was there that it hit him—his *aha* moment. No one was farming this pig in the States. So he took the thing he does well—financing—and he matched it with his passion for food to create a new challenge, a new step—his act two.

Here he was in his late seventies with all the money, cars, and the freedom to retire, but he knew he wasn't done, and he refused to stagnate. Staying on the investment banking path—the well-lit, obvious path—wasn't satisfying anymore. He did what was probably the last thing he'd have imagined as a boy. He started a Mangalica pig farm in the States, and you know what? Now he's the godfather of the scene. It was the challenge he needed to break free from his shackles. And whenever you hear him talk about it, his voice changes—it becomes more alive.

JAMIE KERN LIMA

Jamie was the type of woman who many would have said had it all. She won Miss Washington USA in 1999, she was a contestant on Big Brother (and the last female guest left on the show), she had an MBA from Columbia, she was a journalist, and she was (and still is) gorgeous.

But no one is perfect, and one day, Jamie started losing her eyebrows and gaining weight. It seemed her body was rejecting everything that she used to try to make it go back to so-called normal again. Her physical transformation sparked an interest in makeup that she hadn't had prior, and she began playing around with ways to pencil her eyebrows back in and give her face a more slimming look. She wasn't happy with the products she found in the market—the products claiming to even skin tone didn't even begin to cut it! The brow pencils were a joke, and it was as if the makeup was designed for people with near-flawless skin, the skin she once had. That was her aha moment: there was something missing in the cosmetic industry for people like her, whose eyebrows were falling out, whose lashes were no longer thick, and whose skin had become uneven. In 2008, she launched her own company called IT Cosmetics.

Attempting to sell her line to CVS, she was told she wasn't a fit to sell cosmetics. She didn't give up. Through her persistency, she landed a spot on the Home Shopping Network (HSN). Immediately, her cosmetics disrupted the market—women everywhere who shared Jamie's skin issues were thrilled. IT Cosmetics had become a success, and yet, that was only the breach of things. In 2016, L'Oréal purchased her company for—wait for it—$1.2 billion, and she became the first CEO of any L'Oréal-branded company.

Many people would have told someone like Jamie that she was crushing it in her earlier days. She was a journalist, she both won and hosted Miss Washington USA, she had her MBA, and she was admittedly successful. But she wasn't feeling it internally anymore and pursued the path that was meaningful to her. Instead of stagnating when her body betrayed her, she fought for a solution and to help other women in the same position.

SARAH KAUSS

Sarah, like our other examples, was successful. With an MBA from Harvard, she was working as an accountant at Ernst & Young, but it was her dream to design a water bottle to be sold in Starbucks. What kind of dream was that? Everyone told her she was crazy. There were a million water bottles in the world already, and it would be impossible to get into business with a place as big as Starbucks anyway. Ignoring the naysayers, she moved forward with her design, strategy, and plan.

And then, lightning struck. There she was sitting in Starbucks when she recognized its CEO—there, physically there in the same Starbucks. This was one of those moments, folks. When the opportunity is literally right there, do you run and hide in fear your plan isn't fleshed out enough, do you ask for an appointment for later so you can come back more prepared, or do you pitch your idea right then and there despite how much or how little Joe you've already consumed?

Sarah did not waste the opportunity. She marched right up to Howard Schultz and laid out her idea. "Sit down," he said, and the pitch turned into a full-fledged business meeting, which then turned into a business deal. Starbucks picked up her line, Oprah touted it, and before long, *Forbes* estimated her earnings at $180 million. Today, she's listed as one of America's richest self-made women.

THE NOT-SO-SEXY ROUTE

We can all think of someone who reinvented himself or herself, from the born-again Christian to the midlife-crisis victim. These people change in such a grandiose fashion that we can't help but assume the change won't stick (because it usually doesn't). Additionally, their big acts take such an emotional expense that they exhaust themselves, fall back to where they were, and become less likely to adapt in the future. If that weren't bad enough, society likes to outcast these folks, too. "Oh, Jimmy? Yeah, he's a freak. He quit his job, bought a fancy car, left his wife. He totally lost it." We innately know they didn't futureproof themselves and feel eager to find out how badly it will end.

What about the people who always remained current? The people without Hollywood overnight success stories who took the far-less-sexy route via ten-years-in-the-making stories (a seemingly tortuous time span for our culturally ingrained mindsets that want it all and want it now)? The five examples we discussed took the long-haul route and futureproofed their careers. We all know there is no such thing as overnight anything, especially success.

In the grand scheme of this thing called life, it's the slow-burning fire that gets you through the night, not the quick-to-die flame.

WHAT DO YOU REALLY KNOW ABOUT THAT?

Picture a spectrum with your normal, average, expected experiences on one end and foreign experiences on the other. Do you play on one side of the field? Becoming more strategic means you need to first recognize your position and then learn to expand your assumed role.

Where are you operating: in comfort or with courage? Inspired by a chance witnessing of Brené Brown at a conference (before she became a household name), I started to question my own areas of comfort and how courage served me. In her words, "We can choose courage or we can choose comfort, but we can't have both. Not at the same time."

I was myself, a walking lightning rod at the time, waiting for something to strike—and she did. I will be forever thankful for that phrase in that moment.

Did it just strike you, too?

For an explanation of my own exploration with this and a guide to how you can look at where you are living on this spectrum, mosey on back to try the Courage and Comfort exercise.

Of course, you should check out Ms. Brown, too. She's a badass and game-changer—with great cowboy boots.

The second part behind strategy comes with engaging your senses and forming opinions. We judge others all the time and don't often question where we stand unless for easy items such as politics or religion. Our existing opinions are based on what we've already assumed and rarely do we revisit them, even upon receipt of new information. How many people do you know admit that they were [enter label here] but upon gaining new information, adapted to [enter new label here]? Imagine that. Wouldn't it be lovely? We'd be highly evolved, but instead, we filter new information to fit within our beliefs as opposed to making new opinions. It's how we make sense of the world, and we started doing it at an early age as a coping mechanism to the incessant barrage of information our minds needed to quickly vet and file. To keep evolving, we must reevaluate our old opinions and be open to revising them.

Perhaps the most valuable perspective is the one you don't have yet.

We can easily gut-check our opinions by understanding when we formed them. I made an opinion about divorced families as a child when my best friend's parents divorced, and I saw how sad and difficult it was on him. I only revisited my opinion as an adult when a friend divorced and I saw how much happier it made her and her children. If I had the chance to go back and change the ultracareful, walking-on-eggshells way I treated friends from divorced families throughout my life, I certainly would.

We make judgments because they're convenient. It's the equivalent of cramming for an exam with CliffsNotes; we don't get the full story. If we want the full story, we must evaluate our old opinions with an open, curious mind.

INGREDIENTS EVERYWHERE

Ingredients don't need to be an event. If you're sitting beside someone at the airport, you can simply engage with him and learn something new. Taking small original steps keeps the momentum.

Imagine you're still at the airport and you were delayed. You could sit down and scroll through your usual markets (Costco, aka the media; a convenience store, aka social media), or you could search for a market outside your defaulted norm. I like to buy a magazine that falls outside my knowledge base and interests. Let's say it's *Popular Woodworking* or *Fish & Game*. All I'm doing is reading a magazine, and yet, I engage my emotions in that feeling: *God, do I have to do this?*

I'd rather work than read a magazine outside my interests, but I do it because it's part of my practice. Without fail, I learn something new every time, which becomes useful in the future (in ways I could not have predicted). I couldn't have presupposed reading about how to dovetail a drawer would serve me to better explain something to a client. Or that I could relate to someone I always struggled with after I learned more about fishing.

Instead of turning off and robotically going through life, actively seek new information outside your norm. There's no excuse not to do it every day when it's as simple as reading an article outside your interests. Or a perspective that takes a contrarian angle on something you believe— for example, Fox News versus CNN.

ARE THERE TOO MANY CURATORS IN YOUR KITCHEN?

Facebook algorithms study our patterns and curate based on them. Essentially, social media knows our habits so well that it gives us more of the same. The more we talk about, search, or engage in particular topics, the more we'll see them, and as such, we've unintentionally funneled ourselves into a vortex. All these systems from Facebook to traditional education shell out prescribed worlds, and it's up to us to break from the shackles and expand.

Systems aside, even our friends and communities deepen our funnels. People talk to us about what they know we're interested in to stay on safe and sure ground. We avoid challenging conversations because it's not cool to be a philosopher. It's cool to be a dog or a sheep.

Philosophers are outliers, the thinkers, and the people living in practice. But ask anyone if he wants to be a sheep and he's sure to say no. If you don't want to be a sheep, don't act like one. Go out and challenge your status quo a little bit every day.

Chapter 7

COMMON PITFALLS

Our need for control challenges our ability to expand ourselves and collect new ingredients. In the last chapter, we talked about how we become defensive drivers as adults, how we're eager to dismiss other cars around us as unnecessary or even jerks, and how we stick to our old opinions without strategically revisiting them. While we're using driving metaphors, let's compare our need for control to our reliance on GPS.

When we live life with GPS, we become robots and miss opportunities left and right. We assume we'll get to our destination because someone will tell us when to turn (in fact, that someone will be so precise that he'll tell us five miles leading up to the turn and 250 feet prior). Think about how a GPS recalculates and leads us in the wrong direction. How do you handle that? Do you stop driving toward your dream because you no longer have directions?

While we have our heads down tinkering with the GPS, we could very well miss the woman walking past our car who happens to know the way to Sesame Street. Or we see her walk by, but we don't have the guts to roll down the window and ask a question. We hate to admit we don't know everything and defer to our old tools to avoid emotion. That, my friends, is a pitfall.

A very common pitfall among the most accomplished and successful, those who have mastery in a domain, is to find it *very* hard to feel the pang of the essential student forced out of knowing and into the unknown.

The fact you pulled over may be a pitfall, but pitfalls happen, and it's all about how you handle them. Will you waste forty minutes on your phone trying to find directions, or will you get out of the car and take action? Please don't wait until you're so hungry and desperate to relieve yourself that you finally act—most mammals are capable of more strategy.

WHAT DO YOU CONTROL?

We love to feel in control because it makes us feel safe. We schedule ourselves down to the minute, and deviations from said schedules frazzle us. The result? We become such tightly wound clocks that if so much as a hair gets into our gears, we'll explode.

One of the first exercises I do with my clients is to go through a list of their responsibilities, all their activities, and what comprises their time. I ask them to circle items over which they have complete control and to tear those items out and make a pile with them. Only the uncontrollable items remain, and they'll make a separate pile with those. Which pile do you think is bigger? The truth is, the first grouping hardly makes a pile because we can control only one or two items in life at best. Seeing the difference in physical terms helps remind us of the importance for remaining nimble and adaptable.

We cannot control our lives; therefore, we must be willing to pivot. Living a wristwatch-controlled life guarantees disappointment.

Take the reins off the horses you're not riding by doing the exercise at the back of this book. I guarantee you will break a rule if you do, and if you got this far in this book, you are a natural at rule breaking. It'll be easy and fun as hell. Flip to the back and let's break a rule together with the exercise called Rip and Rank.

WHAT IS A RISK?

Picture kids in the old days pushing an old wheel around the neighborhood with a stick. Effort makes the wheel go; effort is our pursuit. The more effort we put in, the faster it goes, and the steering gets more difficult. With practice, we get better at steering, but we'll never be able to control the terrain, and that's life. Experience (and education) makes the ride smoother, but we're fools to assume the road will remain smooth forever.

Why, then, take risks? Why preemptively alter the smooth ride when the terrain may do that for us? Taking risks keeps us as nimble humans, whereas exerting control keeps us stiff. Risk is opportunity with a bad name tag.

We're introduced to risk as a bad thing and subconsciously filter it out of our world, to play safe. Consequently, we stop witnessing and cling to our old opinions. Yet when someone comes along, goes against the prescription, and experiences wild success, we spite them for it.

What if you look at what you'd traditionally call a risk and consider it an opportunity? How were you introduced to the so-called risk and did that affect your judgment? Sometimes it's all in the delivery. If the waitress gushes about the fried grasshoppers as something you can't die without trying, you're more likely to be swayed than if she offers no opinion or, of course, a distasteful one. Tone, body language, and smirks tell us nearly everything we need to know about someone's opinion before they say a word, and by then, we're already subject to processing the information through their lens.

RISK IS OPPORTUNITY WITH A BAD NAMETAG.
- KR

Your Next Act

Even when you love something, you can be easily manipulated against it. I love music, but if someone were to come to me with a dark tone and incredulous look, and announce, "My God, the Stones, the Who, and Neil Young are getting together for a desert concert. How pathetic! I mean, they're so old; who would want to go to that?" If I'm not totally present or engaged with my emotions, I may blindly agree. What if the friend came to me with an excited tone: "You'll never believe how cool this is!" Now I'm more apt to think it's cool, right? It's up to me to first filter the source, tone, opinion, and bias, then to ask questions. In the first example, I need to ask why the concert is a bad thing for me before I agree with the implication. Are only retired folks allowed to go? Are they going to play only their top songs? Or is it just that my friend doesn't like these groups?

Tune into your real feelings before blindly agreeing, dismissing, or discrediting. One man's risk is another man's opportunity.

JACK BE NIMBLE

We usually think risks are only worth it when they increase stature or profit. Why not embrace a risk (opportunity) to become the most interesting person in the room? Or to maintain relevance or get back in touch with the old, unique you who had individual thoughts and interests?

Or to introduce someone you love to something he's lost touch with? Taking a risk may address all the above *and* increase stature and profit. Don't be so quick to filter risks (opportunities). Your act two doesn't start until you have some new tricks. You can't rest on regurgitating act one.

How should we approach risks? By remaining nimble and open. We allow ourselves to feel differently, and we take the time to reflect. We must stop working from a place of rigidity and control, or we will miss the opportunity in risk's costume, in pursuit of a smooth path. The most common pitfall we'll meet is remaining rigid. Imagine you're standing on the edge of a cliff when someone comes to push you. If you're nimble, you could duck, jump out of the way, or do a whole host of other things. If you're rigid, you're brittle and apt to tumble over. When we assume we know what's coming, we stay planted. We have to stay nimble to thrive.

When standing at the edge of the unknown, the future, which would you prefer to be—nimble or planted?

ONLY THE NIMBLE NEED APPLY

We create balance when we're nimble, which leads to the work-family-life balance question. I'm asked how I manage "it all" ad nauseam. I have three kids and my husband and I are both entrepreneurs, I have a multimillion-dollar business, and I travel the world frequently. We're such black sheep that it makes some nervous just to be near us. How could we possibly balance it all? We're not aliens; we just manage by being nimble.

Recently, I was taken off a flight because my son was ill and couldn't keep his food down. As you can imagine, everyone was irate. The woman in the seat ahead of me said she didn't understand how I could be so unruffled given the situation and that I'm a great mother. While I'll gladly accept the compliment, what's interesting is that she expected me to be irate like everyone else. She was shocked that I wasn't. Of course, I was exhausted, frustrated, and felt awful for my son, but his flu and the airline's decision to kick us off the plane was out of my control. The best I could do was to remain nimble and keep moving forward. I asked myself what I could control. In math terms, I was looking for the common denominator. The only thing I could control was my composure. What good would kicking and screaming do? We were headed off the plane either way, and above all, my son was sick. The point is, the more rigid we are, the worse things get.

Think in terms of who you want to hire: a solutions-focused, nimble, yet capable-of-containing-his/her-composure individual or a rigid person dependent on tight controls? It's not a tough question when put so straightforwardly.

Allow yourself to normalize the stray from status quo. Admit you can't control everything. The very idea that we can is crazy. What good will fearing the boogeyman do you when you did everything possible to keep him out? You'll spend your time circularly by staying in pain and discomfort in an attempt to avoid pain and discomfort— unless you start breaking the cycle today.

The investment in your futureproof strategy is a long-term game. We all want overnight solutions, but remember, they rarely stick. Recognize that what you're doing, even if uncomfortable, will serve you tomorrow. Women go through excruciating pain to have a baby, and refugees flee in search of freedom, not for the discomfort but for the hopes and promises on the other side. We won't go anywhere if we're too worried to take an unclear or uncomfortable path.

THE SHORT GAME

Virtually everyone is (at least somewhat) familiar with the game of golf. You start at the tee box, then work your ball toward the green, hoping to get your ball in the hole. But what do we do when we're impatient? We take a giant swing in hopes of getting a hole in one.

Hole in ones rarely happen, yet we strut out to every game thinking we'll nail one. When we don't get the hole in one, we're so let down that we stop playing well (or altogether). If we just used shorter, smarter strokes over time, we *would* get there. Most importantly, we stay in the game. Something the eighty-five-year-old player knows all too well. He can't hit the big swings anymore, but he still wants to play, so he takes the short strokes. And you know what? Every so often, he'll take fewer strokes than the strong young fools shanking it with their impatient, lavish moves.

There's a clear difference between confidence and competence. We often start with too much confidence and too little competence. Developing competence takes time. Our goal is to have both working for us in equal parts. That way, when the TV crew films our golf swing live, we keep the confidence we need to not get rattled and the competence to play a strong game. Here's the riddle of reality: we are often so comfortable with our competence that we lack confidence. In other words, despite our experience, when the TV crew comes, we botch it.

Clients frequently declare they're not ready for something because they've become so accustomed to being competent and comfortable that taking a risk sounds asinine. "I have too much to lose." Back to the riddle: you can't be competent in what you want to be competent in until you have enough confidence to develop *more* competence. Over time, the two become far too imbalanced, and we need to bring back the equilibrium.

Plot yourself and your career on this spectrum:

Competence ·· Confidence

If you are the kind of person who likes to dive deep and get next-level understanding, take it to the next level with the accompanying exercise.

Feeling over competent is a pitfall because it means we lack the confidence to take risks. We think we've checked off all the big boxes, the "firsts" of our lives, and thus, we're done. We got laid for the first time, we moved out, graduated, got married, got a career. Now we ought to keep things smooth sailing, right? Brake pumping leads to the itch. Once we run out of questions, boxes, and ideas, we're naturally going to wonder what's next because we're bored. We played all the easy holes; now it's time for the interesting ones.

Once on the plateau, many disguise old activities as new opportunities in hopes of feeling satisfied again. Maybe they refurbish rooms in their house they refurbished a couple of years ago. Or in an attempt to shake things up, they go to Turks and Caicos like they do every year, this time with another couple. There, they'll probably overdo the margaritas in desperate search of wild fun. These people are close, but they're missing the mark. They're up for the action, but they've stopped being curious enough to expand their worlds, so they end up doing repeat actions. We'll never get the same high from redoing what was once a first.

Remember, we don't control the terrain, so no amount of control will keep us safe. Risks are opportunities with a bad name. Stay nimble and don't shy away from opportunities just to live on repeat. Short strokes every day keep you moving forward—they keep you in the game.

Chapter 8

MORE AHA MOMENTS

We all want moments of divine inspiration. There we are, sitting at our desks going through our routines and hoping the clouds will part and...Hallelujah! We're struck with a brilliant idea. Nice try. When was the last time you had an amazing idea at your desk? We know ideas surface elsewhere such as in the car or during a conversation, yet we stay at our desks, frustrated.

The futureproof lifestyle invites aha moments, which are the little cracks that shift your perspective and lead to new ideas. The aha moment is the gunshot signaling a marathon. It may not be the winning step across the finish line; rather, it's the grand and beautiful clue on how to get there. Sparking aha moments alleviates our internal pressure to produce winning concepts on the spot. Not all ideas win; some are just arrows pointing you in the right direction.

MODERNIZING THE INNOVATOR'S DILEMMA

Clayton M. Christensen's *The Innovator's Dilemma* discusses how costly it is to be the innovator and the one to vet new ideas and create new technology. Consider how much more money the first person to invent the computer had to spend than those who came after. Sadly, it's easier (and cheaper) to copy. But the copycat fails to cling to the first-movers advantage, the market share gained by being first (particularly when holding a patent). While expendable budgets and immense teams may help you innovate and get there first, they can also slow you down. I want to dispel the old dilemma and give it a modern spin: you can innovate on little budget and without a giant team.

Earlier, we discussed Betamax versus VHS, and for those of you who remember (and perhaps had a Betamax), you'll know Betamax was not only first but it also had better technology. Yet it was VHS (the company without the first-mover's advantage) that won the market share. Why? They took time to adapt and offer the public what they wanted—diversity. You don't need to be the person who invented coding when there are spin-off opportunities galore.

The tools and information we need to innovate have never been more democratized. *The Innovator's Dilemma* was a corporate dissection of an innovator's necessities and doesn't reflect today's opportunity. We no longer need to be part of a giant corporation to win at the innovation game, to change ourselves, our industry, or even the world. You don't need to do a hundred thousand things differently. Look at Uber; it did two things differently: it changed how you order a cab and how the cab is supplied. Now it's up to Uber to keep adapting to stay in the game. Facebook started as an invite-only community and over time adapted to let everyone in. Airbnb combined social networking with hotel booking and revolutionized the way we travel.

What *The Innovator's Dilemma* needs to modernize is a dose from Kobi Yamada's children's book, *What Do You Do with an Idea?* His book explains that an idea needs nourishment and confidence to grow and become bigger than us. You don't need a team and budget to prove your idea has worth. So what do you need—what are the seeds for innovation?

THE SIX REQUIREMENTS FOR INNOVATION

1. Trust
2. Freedom
3. Intuition
4. Training
5. Being present
6. Translating

Trust is vital to innovation. Without it, we risk questioning and doubting an idea. When we fall into the doubt trap, we fail to expand the idea's potential, and we kill the chance for innovation. It's easier to assume an idea has been done before or convince yourself it won't work than it is to groom and evolve it. Keep the idea to yourself at first to build trust and confidence. Later, involve those you trust to help you out of the depths of doubt. Your idea is like a baby; it needs your care and devotion.

The second necessary component for innovation is **freedom**. Ideas need the space and time to evolve, shift, and expand. We've all been struck with what we think is the genius panacea, but sleeping on it, poking, and prodding the idea will test its merit and potential.

Intuition is our overlooked secret weapon. We've been taught to seek insights and scientific data to prove our ideas work before committing—the equivalent to the chicken-before-the-egg conundrum. We rely on what algorithms know while dismissing the fact algorithms use data we gave it (not to mention we designed the damn thing!). It's like driving with your eyes on the rearview mirror. True innovation changes the paradigm, and therefore, we cannot rely on data, because the data isn't yet available. Remember, intuition is the culmination of all your experience and knowledge. It's your sixth-sense-like wisdom; tune in and trust it.

We need adequate **training** to translate our innovation to the world. Our training builds the vocabulary in our skillset's language and allows us to explain our knowledge to the world. Training is necessary to turn esoteric concepts into clarity.

We must be **present**. Before you dismiss being present as new wave or hippyish, think of being present as actively witnessing what's happening—in other words, being reliable. If called to the stand, you'd recall a scene with surety because you're alert when you drive as opposed to cruising about in highway hypnosis.

Translation is the final stage for your innovation, the time you bring your baby out from hiding and share it with the world. Don't get stuck worrying your idea will be stolen or judged. Remember, your idea is still your baby and thrives best with you. Allow it to go through its ugly phase, nurture it, and care for it until it's ready for the world; when it is, it's time to use your training and translate it. The ugliest babies often turn out to be supermodels.

Your next thing is an evolution creating a revolution. Act two takes time to hatch, develop, go through the awkward stage, build confidence, and prove itself capable and worthy of your effort.

BRINGIN' IT BACK TO THE OLD SCHOOL

Philosophers such as Aristotle made it cool to question. They approached life with an open mind as opposed to predetermining outcomes. Playing allows us to do the same thing. When kids can't find their favorite toys in the sandbox, they make do with what's there even if that means using a leaf, a dead butterfly, and a truck. They'll use these makeshift tools and without judgment or presupposition. Kids work in the height of creativity when not given limitations, rules, or instructions. Over time, we're taught the opposite approach, which has dampened our ability to innovate. We must remain curious to gain wisdom.

To unlock our next act, we must tap into our unique ingredients—even bad experiences—and identify what we possess that cannot be imitated. What differentiates you versus the twenty-some other people with the same training or language and solid work experience? To be exceptional, you must make an exception to your own rules. What is it about you that can't be imitated?

First, think about what you believe makes you unique, then ask a friend. It's that simple—and that hard.

We've been conditioned to live in our own little worlds and compartmentalize what we learn. Cataloging is a dangerous habit because it blinds us to possible interconnectedness among concepts, people, and things. Think about how we introduce ourselves using labels and silos. When you're asked to introduce yourself without applying these terms, you stumble—in other words, you stumble over your very identity! If we're not in the practice of making connections, we close ourselves off to innovation. Sometimes innovation is nothing more than two disparate things colliding. Steve Jobs didn't create communication or phones; he made the communication medium an entertaining experience. Essentially, he combined a variety of tools into the meat grinder to make the iPhone.

YOU WANNA TRY THAT AGAIN?

We already discussed that we don't need an endless budget to spur innovation, just like we don't need to skydive in Brazil to have an experience. Experiences are everywhere and out for the taking. In fact, you can re-experience something you've already done and gain new tools. I have a friend who wondered how she'd manage to stock new ingredients when she travels nonstop for work and has very little free time. Why not approach something as mundane as how you go to the airport as a new adventure? You can re-experience the drive by going a different way, taking a cab if you usually drive, or vice versa. We all have certain ways we introduce ourselves, eat our lunch, or even sit on a plane. When you make simple adaptations to these defaults, you stock new ingredients.

What in your regular routine can you slightly alter? What if it's just re-experiencing how you walk down your neighborhood streets? For one client, we started by adapting a new way of getting dressed. Instead of dressing in the morning, I asked her to write down a list of five attributes she wanted her ensemble to reflect the night before and to choose her outfit that night. The adaptation took little effort, but the exercise completely transformed her morning, and as a result, she re-experienced the entire day differently. The shift affected her attitude, which ultimately changed how others perceived her for the better.

Small adaptations build momentum and lead to more positive adaptations. Better yet, they remind us we are alive dammit, and we are, in **choice**, far more than our routine lives would have us aware. You have a choice.

RIDE THE WAVE

It's time to dust off your old science skills and imagine a sound wave. There's a wave moving up and down the way you'd imagine a heartbeat wavelength moving up and down on a monitor. Now overlay another wave, one passing at a different interval. It's as if there were two heartbeat waves beating at different times. Eventually,

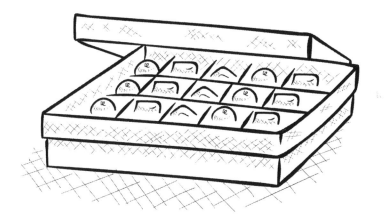

YOU HAVE A CHOICE.

#YourNextAct

the waves cross; we'll consider this a place and experience in history. Depending on which wave you're riding, you'll see the meeting point differently. If you're the upward-facing wave, you'll have a totally different viewpoint than the downward-traveling wave.

Apply the wave example to something as simple as passing the same person at the same times every weekday. You witness a guy at the same location, at the same time, wearing a suit and holding a coffee. What if you changed the timing of your so-called wave so that when your lines cross, you see Mr. Coffee doing something differently, which makes you see him differently, too.

We can apply the concept to re-experiencing life. If you bungee jumped at eighteen and again at thirty-eight, you'd have two different experiences and emotions. The slightest shift can change our perspective of the world without imposing a single threat or requiring anyone else to change. Don't worry about how others see you. Simply witness, reengage, and re-experience even the most basic aspects of your life. It will point you to the questions you seek and answers you need to break through the stagnation fog over time.

TIP ME OVER AND POUR ME OUT

Everyone is different, which means some of us will feel

differently immediately after employing a futureproof mindset and making daily adaptations to kick-start act two. For others, it will take more time. If you fall into the second category, don't fret. Futureproofing is a long-term game, and we can't expect to wake up and see life in living color; we need to build momentum. Just as we didn't get to status quo overnight, getting ourselves out won't be immediate either. There will, however, come a tipping point, a moment where things change enough for the world to take note. Often, the tipping point feels retroactive for us because we're actively pushing forward. By the time others recognized my client's positive internal changes after she'd altered the way she got dressed, she'd already been going about it for some time. There's a scale of sensitivity involving the tipping point; some have deeper dependence on external feedback than others and won't feel the difference until they get to that point. Wherever you fall on said scale, you must keep at the practice and rest assured your adaptations are valuable even before others notice and validate them.

The tipping point can feel exhilarating, but it poses a threat. It's tempting to get swept into the tipping point's validation high and relish in the moment, but don't relish so long that you get stuck on your plateau again and stop building new steps to climb. *Box checked! I ran a half marathon, lost thirty pounds, and now I'm done!* That's fine if you made exercising a daily practice and you're continuously trying experiences—it's *not* OK if you go back to your old ways. Stagnation waits with open arms; don't fall into its trap. Keep your momentum with sustainable daily adaptations to your defaulted norms.

DO YOU UNDERSTAND WHAT I'M SAYING?

How are experience and training related? Training is the language that enables us to translate our experiences. Simply having a hammer doesn't make you a carpenter any more than having an MBA makes you a businessperson. Your skills won't get you very far if you can't translate them.

When I speak at MBA convocations, my message isn't always immediately welcomed. "Congratulations," I'll say to the sea of happy faces, the moms and dads, and people who dropped a few hundred thousand on a degree. "You're graduating just like all the other people around you. You've leveled up and become mediocre at the same time." The faces in the crowd melt. The parents ask themselves what the hell kind of address I'm giving. Where's the inspiration? That's when I tell them the MBA degree doesn't make them businesspeople; it only means they understand and speak the business language. But if they can translate that skill and use their own unique tools to create a cool new business, they'll differentiate from the pack, lift out of the base level that is mediocrity, and make a difference.

Until you use that hammer, you're not a carpenter. Use your unique tools to translate your skills, or you're just another person speaking the same boring language. When we operate at the level of worthy colleagues or opponents, what made us "qualified" and "special" before now becomes the table stakes.

IMPOSTER'S SYNDROME

After we got a $5,000 piece of art with wedding money, I was pumped about the investment and statement it would make in my home. That was until I visited one, two, make that *three* of my best friends' homes and saw a similar piece of art. Talk about buzz kill; I'd bought nothing more than a reproduction. The artist knew this imagery sold well and made the same thing over and over to the point that no one will buy her work now. Her brilliance made her tremendously successful, and yet in adherence to that singular moment of brilliance, she made herself obsolete.

When we reach the pinnacle of our careers, we're prone to imposter's syndrome. In most cases, we're fully aware we're doing the same work as everyone else and that at any given moment, someone may call us out on it, yet we struggle to break from the rut.

We don't find ourselves with imposter syndrome because we're not capable of innovating; it's because we're playing safe. Playing it safe, even at a highly competent level, makes us replaceable. What differentiates you in the great big room of successful people? How will you be the original in a room of reproductions? Strip away everyone's credentials and you're left with an individual's experiences as a means of distinguishing. So what the hell have you done lately? If you haven't done anything interesting, what will you have to say? And if you're fluent in only one language, how many people can you talk to?

Curate new ingredients every day so you don't rip off tried-and-true work as if it's new. Without fresh ingredients, your work will always be stale.

WHAT'S YOUR IP WORTH?

We used to need vast sums of money and huge teams to develop intellectual property (IP). Now, both you alone and your organization can innovate for a lot less money and with fewer people. How you gather and process your experiences is essentially your way of patenting IP. Your value is found in your unique ingredients; without them, you're a reproduction and, honestly, not all that valuable.

It costs nothing to protect your patent (your IP), because no one processes experiences the same way as you. In other words, your tools are unique to the world! Gathering ingredients and honing your ability to translate them is what increases your value. Developing your IP is the next level in the business of your life. If we all open the same shop on the same street and sell the same shit at the same price, how great will our business be? We'll be the status quo person wondering why our profits stagnate.

From a corporate level, organizations should desire those who develop their own IP, the type of people who have something interesting to say about what they did over the weekend versus people who said their weekend was "OK" every time you asked them, or worse, people who were chained to their desk all weekend. Unfortunately, many traditional organizations developed antibodies to these types of people, and I'd like to challenge them to eliminate these outdated antibodies. It's possible you need to remove a disease in the organization. Once the disease is gone, recognize the people who think for themselves and assign them to an innovation lab if you don't have other roles for them. These people are like stem cells, and within them, there's a cell capable of adapting in a way that will solve whatever problem your business may encounter.

Organizations traditionally thrive on certainty and structure, as do the people within them. Embedding the stem cells (innovators) can pose a challenge in that the original unit may want to reject them. Companies wanting to innovate must normalize the free radicals. They must be cognizant that tenured employees often band like militaries ready to attack introducers for fear they'll steal their jobs or disrupt routine. That's why it's crucial that company leaders introduce the innovators transparently and assure the original unit these free radicals are not coming in, because certainty is no longer valued. The company needs to welcome innovation for the good of everyone involved; otherwise, the company will certainly perish and cease to employ them. After all, stagnation is a sickness.

When companies bring innovators in, many existing employees struggle to trust them. Without diplomas proving their worth, they're deemed ambiguous and unworthy. We want proof of innovation, but that brings us back to the chicken-before-the-egg conundrum—which is why we only see courageous leaders supporting outliers with strong IP before said outliers' IP is proven worthy by the rest of the world.

Are you a strong enough leader to breed innovators? What's stopping you from allowing these people and ideas into your corporation? Are you confident you can shepherd innovation? It starts with you.

DO WHATEVER THE FUCK YOU WANT

Whether in an organization or your own life, everything

starts with you. Remember, the cost to protect your IP is zero; it's yours alone, and no one can take it. On the flip side, the cost to keep it protected by not exposing, engaging, or developing it is the difference between your default future and the future you want. It's immeasurable and only each individual person can feel the pain of that truth.

So there you are. You are free and ultimately you can do whatever you want. You can do nothing; that's fine, but just don't expect to be relevant for too long or to live richly and enjoy as many acts as you want in your life on this stage called earth. You can get overexcited and make big, fast changes, but remember our midlife-crisis victim—vast, abrupt changes don't stick. The evolved approach is highly strategic and backed by science. Science tells us how the brain works, and the world's innovators demonstrated how strategy works. This book defines the strategy for you but does not presume to fill in all your blanks and set you on your merry way. It's up to you to make daily adaptations, be nimble, curious, and ready to leave your default. I don't know what your default is, so it's up to you to understand and break free from it—or not. Because ultimately, you can do whatever the fuck you want. You're free.

But hey, you picked this book up for a reason. You don't want to stay at the train station and watch everyone speed by, so just get on the damn train already.

WHAT DOES YOUR LIFE LOOK LIKE IN TERMS OF COFFEE?

There will be days when status quo is more appealing than engaging even the smallest adaptation. If you can't drive a different way to work or order a different coffee at this point in your life, you may as well map out how many years you expect to live. If I want to live to ninety-seven (then I have fifty-seven years to go), and I drink an average 1.5 coffees per day, that gives me 31,207 coffees—or 31,207 opportunities to do something differently.

You're not a huge corporation; you're one person. Your mass is small, which means you can build momentum quickly. All you have to do is start. Pick a direction and go.

SUPERSTAR PANEL

Imagine if Henry Ford came back and when asked his advice as to what today's society should make, he said, "Keep on with the trucks." We know he wouldn't advise us to keep doing the same thing, because he was an innovator. He'd be far more apt to tell us to create an incredibly fast underwater vessel or something we cannot imagine.

If we put all the brilliant people we can think of on a panel (from Abraham Lincoln to Einstein) and showed them how our current system functions, do you think they'd recommend we continue with it (i.e., our box-checking, hoop-jumping system)? They wouldn't, because they didn't follow that method. They broke the mold and created what they dared envision. They didn't presuppose or sit back as the world changed. They pushed forward to *make* the world change. They were exceptional. So are you, remember?

What's your aspiration? What do you want to build? When you're playing Monopoly and you have Boardwalk, and you're ruling the game board, what else are you striving for? Will you keep going around and around the board of life until you're bored to tears, or will you devise a new game?

EXERCISES

The futureproof lifestyle is about instigating daily adaptations, remaining nimble, and questioning your default. Futureproofers witness life and their environment; they invite innovation and aha moments. You're on the game board, and it's time to take action through practice.

I welcome you to visit the book site at SuccessHangover. com where you'll find a community of new and tenured futureproofers and act two, three, four, Xers alike, all sharing their experiences. There, you'll also find the exercises included in this book and more—podcasts and tools to help you measure and quantify your futureproofing progress.

Like I said in the beginning of the book, it's up to you whether or not you want to do the work, but I suspect if you want to ignite your next act, screw your status quo and feel alive again, you will. I'm also guessing that as you do, you might have questions, and you may want to seek a community of others like you. It's important to get out from between these sheets of paper and into the world. Your work will take you from feeling stuck on your own plane into the excitement, freedom, and opportunities, which derive from blasting into the universe of possibility.

I'll see you out there, virtually @kelseyramsden and SuccessHangover.com, and personally, if you choose to email me at Kelsey@SuccessHangover.com.

There is a moment in every dawn when light floats, there is the possibility of magic. Creation holds its breath.

—DOUGLAS ADAMS, *THE HITCHHIKER'S GUIDE TO THE GALAXY*

THE PIÈCE DE RÉSISTANCE

When I was young, I wanted to be a performer, and I asked my parents to put me in drama. Somehow, I ended up taking piano lessons instead of debuting my imagined dramatic skills on stage. Over time, my dream fizzled in the corner (cue the womp, womp here). Years later, I veered further and further from my glamorous dream of being on stage by exploring a different passion (drum-roll please): working with numbers. Yes, I became that geek happy to crank away, alone in a room for hours on end. I was a workhorse feeding off what society told me was good money and ego—until one day, I got hungry for more. I was sick of what they were feeding me. I needed to escape the cell I'd unintentionally locked myself in and embrace something new.

After I won Canada's Top Female Entrepreneur of the Year award the first time, the CEO of Mabel's Labels invited me for lunch (which was huge because as a mother, I was obsessed with Mabel's Labels). Over a beer and salad, she told me I'd make a great speaker. I immediately rejected the idea; it was absurd. I was simply a workhorse. What would I talk about and who would care?

As fate would have it, I received an invitation to do a TEDx talk just two days later. It felt like a sign; how the hell could I say no? I'm naturally a gambler and open to challenges but still—to go from having given zero public talks to delivering a TEDx talk was outright ninja level. The only PowerPoint presentations I'd given were for MBA school and most included assumptions and graphs made the night before. So this opportunity challenged my set of rules—broke them completely actually—and I agreed to do it. Of course, to stay calm, I told myself I'd botch it and go back to my old life immediately afterward, despite the inner voice whispering, *Maybe this is going to be really cool; maybe you're meant to do this.*

As it turned out, people liked my talk; in fact, they loved it. Sometimes what we resist turns out to be what we're best at. I'd unearthed a long protected and nearly forgotten childhood dream and now I was exposed. I could keep pushing forward, return to my safe plateau, or I could and *did* push forward.

I stood out as a speaker because I was never taught to speak and never took courses on it. People tell me they sense I'm truly present during my talks, not just a person standing behind a podium rattling off words, and they're right. It's my practice to be present, to witness, to adapt to the moment. I don't check boxes when I speak, which is why I'll never give the same talk twice.

Sometimes the path leads us back to the place we started. We may end up choosing the original path we wanted to explore, but now we're far more prepared for the journey.

DON'T SIT BACK

Having a new aspect to my life and career opened another chance to improve myself, and that excited me. I didn't get defensive when given advice for public speaking; I embraced it. I was intrinsically motivated, the type of motivation we want in our children and employees so we don't have to extrinsically bribe them to perform. I stopped searching for the bigger high, the bigger award, the grander profile, and more money. I finally understood the old adage about life being about the journey rather than the destination. Talk about an aha moment.

I will always remain curious about what's next, who I am now, where to go, and how to improve. When you're in the futureproof practice, everything feels like an opportunity. It took a long time to learn great things happen a lot; they happen every day. Some experiences will become great business ideas, solutions, and opportunities. Some of the experiences I'll remember in the dying days of my life.

When you embrace a futureproof lifestyle, you'll get so good at being present and so open to opportunities and aha moments that the pressure lifts. Yes, you still need to be exceptional, but when you're living the practice, challenges become more enjoyable and attainable. I will always keep striving to make each performance better than the last. It's what keeps me from becoming an imposter. Futureproofers don't reproduce their work. They stay in the momentum and swim in ideas. They live rich. They feel alive again and again and again.

I'M NOT LIKE THAT, AM I?

We've all joked about our parents or grandparents being out of touch, most likely during the blissful years when we thought we were invincible and would never get old. No one intends to become old, just like no one intends to fall behind and become obsolete. The process doesn't happen overnight, but there comes a day when you realize younger people are referencing technology you haven't embraced—and that the older generation you used to reference is now gone. We may separate ourselves from the younger generations at work and in our personal lives because it's easier to say we can't relate to them and cling to our old ways. But the stick-to-our-safe-ways practice decreases our value and leads to obsolescence.

The cliché "If you're not growing, you're dying" has never been truer. The longer you wait to adapt, the more trains you miss. Get on board by doing something small and easy today, and something small and easy again tomorrow. That's how the lifestyle becomes sustainable. We know it doesn't work when we hit the gym like a maniac on January 2. Small steps are sustainable and build momentum.

Remember that the social component of sharing experiences is vital to embedding the experiences as new ingredients. It's as simple as trying a new coffee and telling someone about it. You don't need to announce to the world you're taking part in a new futureproof lifestyle. "Ahem, I'm trying a half-caff soy latte with caramel chocolate éclair drizzle as part of a social experiment. May I tell you about it?" No. Treat it as your own covert operation at first. You need to tell only one person about your experiences. Once you've built momentum, the world will take note, and that's the tipping point.

While applying these principles in your business, you need to apply them in your personal life. If you're reading in the context of business alone, I unfortunately do have to tap you on the shoulder and whisper in your ear that it starts with you. If you're not making adaptations in your personal life, it's going to be very difficult for you to go along with the evolution that is coming in your business. It's also going to be difficult for you to correctly identify the right people to bring along. Flashy Jill who skydives and feeds gators may have cool experiences, but if she hasn't perfected her language, she's not the person you want on your team. You need to get into the futureproof practice yourself to identify others living it.

The sum of every person's experiences is different. I can never claim to be like you; therefore, I cannot tell you exactly what to do to move up the ladder, be happy, and live the life of your dreams. I can only help you use deductive reasoning to look for clues. Don't expect to hit out of the park as soon as you start futureproofing, because remember, we're talking about the unknown future, which means we don't even know where the park is yet. Follow your interests in a way that engages your emotion and makes you vulnerable, and remember to witness what's happening around you without presupposing outcomes. We can't predict the future; we can only prepare for it.

You are only one person. Your mass is small compared to an organization; small adaptations will build velocity for you quickly. Start going in the right direction toward your future. Stop and ask yourself what's one small thing outside your default you can do now? Will you go out and do it?

HOLLER BACK

I would love to hear from you and learn about your experiences futureproofing. I'll be your wingman until you've made futureproofing such a part of your life that you become another's wingman. By living the futureproof lifestyle, you create a world of people embracing the same mindset, albeit in a way unique to them. Ingredient collectors attract other ingredient collectors; before you know it, you'll be around so many that you can't help but collect new ingredients. Drop me a note when you visit SuccessHangover.com (there is a notes section especially for this purpose), and we'll have a free potluck party with all the global and universal insights we can share.

It seems crazy, I know. I've got hundreds of emails to read and respond to, on top of the already hellish task of email management (a nut I have never fully cracked), but this is a selfish pursuit, and I will openly and happily admit that. I have something to learn from you and your experience; you just haven't given me the opportunity to do it yet. I get high on life when you share with me. I am, after all, a creator who deeply values intimate connection. And what can provide a more intimate connection than daily sharing of who we are, the adaptations we have underway, and the dreams we are creating. I might be inspired by your story or see an opportunity through your experience, and have thoughts I've never had before. This is my drug, you see; it's what makes my world go around.

EXIT STAGE RIGHT

Bravo, you're here, which means you want to *ignite your next act, screw status quo, and feel alive again.* Now it's time to activate your experience by sharing your stories with #YourNextAct because I can't wait to learn from you—to see how you screwed the status quo and are setting the stage for your next act: feeling very much alive again.

Bonus Chapter

THE FUTUREPROOF APPROACH TO PARENTING

This chapter is provided to give those who are parents or leaders in the lives of youth some extra insight and ideas on how to apply the concepts within the book to another area of our lives—in this case, to **parenting**.

I know that not everyone who reads this book will be a parent, so I have included a portion of the chapter here so you can get a taste. If you like it, you can easily get the full chapter over at the book's home on the web at www. SuccessHangover.com.

Let me start this chapter with full disclosure: I'm not a parenting expert, but I am a parent. Additionally, I was luckily afforded very nurturing parents who raised two children with track records of exceptional success—not just monetarily but also in their lives and relationships (if I do say so myself). In this chapter, I'm giving you my perspective on raising a freethinking, exceptional child. I'd also like to note that when I mention "my" kids, it is only to differentiate them from kids in general and not to place them on any kind of podium. Now, let's get to it.

It's time to go down memory lane and think about your good ol' school days. How much of your education do you recall? Big question, I know, but think about it. From all those years, books, lessons, and lectures, what can you truly recall right now? Within that—however much you pulled— let me ask you this: where and when did you learn it?

I'll postulate your memories correspond to three things:

1. **Emotional moments.** (I remember the pain I felt when struggling in calculus)
2. **Action-based learning.** Creating and/or collaborating on a project (I remember Highway One goes from one side of Canada to the other and passes the CN Tower because I had to write a report on it. I also loved the teacher who gave it an added emotional element).
3. **Reality-based learning.** Skills used in real life (I know two plus two and use this skill to make change).

Here's the problem: the traditional education system

isn't enough to arm our children with the tools needed to become what will result in success in the future or to make them innovative leaders; success in the future will require them to be freethinkers and innovators. And it's up to us to apply the 3E Method to raise curious, free-thinking innovators. While I promise this chapter is not intended to discredit education, I do want to identify where the outdated educational system falls short and risks becoming a default experience, even a babysitter. Think about it: our children will spend twelve to eighteen years in education, but how much will they get from it? You're not alone if you're underwhelmed, so let's fill in the void. By applying the futureproof approach to parenting, you maximize your children's learning, prepare them for success and happiness, and strengthen your relationship in the process. After all, we want our kids to rise above status quo, right? We want them to be exceptional.

Sadly, as a society, we've veered far from Aristotle's definition of school, especially when considering the word *school* comes from the Greek word for leisure. His peripatetic school (peripatetic literally meaning "to walk about"—the way Aristotle did as he lectured) was centered on philosophy and science. It was cool to think and question, to be curious. Much has changed.

In Ken Robinson's beloved TED talk (viewed no less than forty-five million times), "Do Schools Kill Creativity?" he explains that today's educational system was designed to serve the Industrial Revolution. Students were thrown into the grinder like cogs, told what to do, and taught not to question but rather to follow rules. It worked extremely well in providing society what it needed at that time—factory and desk workers meant to repeat the same actions over and over. Once out of school, it was the most responsible people who would ascend the ladder, and managers were less leaders and thinkers than they were rule followers. We're all well aware that we've moved far beyond the Industrial Revolution. We plunged into the information revolution and are now moving toward a robotic revolution. Why, then, are we still using an educational box-checking system designed for the Industrial Revolution?

When kids excel in our educational system, it does not ensure they'll succeed, be prepared, or become innovators. It's more probable to assume they'll make mediocre mid-level workers. I think it's safe to assume that's not what you're envisioning for your child.

WHAT TO ASK?

There's no better person to expand your child's education than you. You can develop their mindset at the most basic level by the way you communicate with them before and after school. When I send my kids to school, I tell them to be kind and respectful, and to witness. I encourage them to ask good questions, to be curious, and expose themselves. When they come home, instead of asking them how their day was (which elicits a one-word answer) or what they had for lunch (so simple a monkey could answer it), I ask them what surprised them or what happened that was unexpected, and then I keep probing for more.

We don't want our children to spend their days checking boxes and regurgitating information (i.e., behaving like well-trained seals); we know that won't serve them in the long term. After all, our kids can Google just about any answer they'll need, which is why it's crucial we encourage and teach them to stay curious.

Google cannot tell me what I'm curious about, and staying curious is my X factor—my special sauce. Because admit it, there is no competition or reward for being the best Google searcher. And if there is, I don't want to win it.

YOU AGAINST THE WORLD

Sure, everyone wants to be an entrepreneur, but what does that word really mean? My fellow board members for the entrepreneurship counsel at the top university in Canada discuss this question frequently. The word has become overglorified; everyone wants to be an entrepreneur, yet universities struggle with how to define or teach the skill. Entrepreneurs are nothing more than freethinkers who take action. Instead of teaching how to be an entrepreneur, business schools should teach leadership skills to freethinkers.

Freethinkers are curious, they investigate, and they adapt. The standard education model tells us we need numbers, statistics, and cases to prove concepts. In our society, technology moves so quickly that we no longer even have the math or history to prove most theories. Theories are not set in the future, or the history is so short that we can't create the stats for them in the way that formerly justified our actions. Freethinkers don't need the stats to keep moving.

Traditional training teaches us to hit the brakes and seek more information. Remember the Step Function Model from chapter 2? That's what's happening—our kids don't know how to build a new step and progress. Additionally, today's kids aren't taught to witness their environments, and ultimately, they're insecure. They're not armed with the necessary tools to adapt and respond; worse, these skills are never even addressed.

When I graduated high school in 1994, my dad told me I'd be competing in a global environment. His words didn't compute until I was in MBA school and saw how many international students there were; I was no longer competing with people from my own country. Since then, the competitive global market has increased exponentially. Far more educational systems around the world have caught up with the Western standards or surpassed them. Moreover, students have far more access to information than they once did, which allows them to circumvent the system. We find people who started their own (incredibly successful) businesses when they were teens and who never needed to go to MBA school. The potential for people to bolster both their credibility and competitive ability on the job frontier has democratized tenfold. Our kids will compete with the world. So what differentiates your child from another? Google, as in the company, doesn't care if your child comes from a great family in San Francisco; Google wants to hire the kid who's going to solve problems.

Companies such as Ernst & Young have stopped hiring based on the old checkbox list. Formerly, their new hires came from one of five MBA schools, whereas today, they no longer require an MBA. Large organizations woke up and recognized they weren't buying all the ingredients they needed. They were hiring vanilla cake bakers, which didn't give them the tools for success in the long haul, nor did it do anything to differentiate them from all the other firms stocked with the top vanilla cake bakers from the same top schools.

Our first step as parents is to recognize where value lies. We're setting our kids up for failure and significant strife by keeping quantifiable, box-checking skills at the top of the hierarchy. We must create a new checkbox, a new metric, and transform education by teaching our children to be nimble, curious, freethinking adapters. Freethinking lessons don't come with a prescription or a grade, but they will serve your kids in the long run.

How many kids out there thought they were dumb because they earned Cs in a world telling them only As prove otherwise. Getting As doesn't guarantee the life it once did. In fact, the more you cling to the idea of straight As, the more likely you'll raise a hoop jumper great at regurgitating information. Focusing on grades only sells our children short. The world expects As; it's the new basic level, because the world is moving so fast that it can't tell you what else it wants or needs. That's why we must get predictive, adaptive, and intuitive to not only keep up but also get ahead.

Every day is an opportunity to offer an experience that will deepen your relationship with your children *and* prepare them for the future. What will you do today? What about tomorrow and the day after that? Your answer to that question is a major predictor in your child's future success. So how will your child measure up?

To get the rest of this chapter, visit www.SuccessHangover.
com.

GLOSSARY

- **act two.** For those who achieved, looked around, and wondered, *Is this it?*, and still wanted more or potentially something else entirely.
- **default future.** Where you're headed if you make no adaptations to your life as it is right now.
- **exceptionalism.** To live above status quo in a satisfied, successful, and alive state.
- **futureproofing.** An above-average ability to adapt to and/or create solutions for unknown future obstacles and opportunities.
- **ingredients.** New experiences, tools, knowledge, and people.
- **relevant.** Purposeful and influential across genres of contemporary interest.
- **rich.** The wholeness of self in relation to soul-driven satiation—a wholeness of self.
- **shelves.** Metaphor for one's knowledge and ingredients as if they were stored like books in a library. (Note: most people if not only, most readily, use their eye-level shelf.)

KNOWN AND UNKNOWN CONTRIBUTORS

If your name appears here, you were directly responsible for at least one line, one insight, or one lifetime with me that has come together to form this book.

Alice Miller
Aristotle
Auntie Flo
Barbie Ross
Bob Dorf
Brené Brown
Bruce Kitsch
Cameron Arskey
Cameron Herold
Claire Monachon
Courtney Lochner

Don Ennis
Doug Brackmann
Drumstick
Elliot Walker
Emily Gindlesparger
Esther Kitsch
Fraser Johnson
Goose
Gord Downie
Hot Buns
Jamie Rea
James Murphy
James Tonn
Jayson Gaignard
Jen Hansard
Jennifer Stovel Mellon
Jennifer Zimmerman
Julie Ellis
Karen Hanna
Kendra Neufeld
Krista Stogryn
Laura Reitveld
Liz Abbott
Marg Ramsden
Margaret Whitley
Michael Ross
Mike Turner
Navada Taylor

Renee Geraghty
Ria Kitsch
Robin Wortley
Robyn Watt
Rooster
Rudy Kitsch
Seth Godin
Shep Gordon
Steven Pressfield
Steven Tyler
Thomas Petty
Todd McClellan
Trent Kitsch
Tricia Mumby
William Nelson
You

NOTES AND
EXERCISES

.

DEFAULT FUTURE

- **Future.** Time regarded as still to come
- **Default.** When no alternative is specified by the user

This one is straightforward and likely one of the paramount reasons you are reading this book. You are capable, successful in many ways, and yet you feel stuck or lifeless in your pursuits at the moment. You likely look to the future and recognize the status quo leads to a default future that isn't too appealing; it might even be appalling. *Shit.*

You are also reading this book because only the driven do. Ambitious people simply don't settle for status quo long. They thirst to take action, to shift from stalled into a state of ignition. Ambitious people want to get going. So let's do it.

This isn't a test; no one will peek at your answers. Just write down what comes to you, as there is no "right" and it's not permanent.

If you don't want to write it here, you can print a copy off at the book site, SuccessHangover.com, and keep your paper here looking pristine enough to share this copy with someone you know could use it after you've read it.

If you are serious about progress, a fun experiment is to complete this now, then again after you have read the book and done all the other exercises. Really, the proof of this book is in that pudding: it's what you get out of it, measurable, actionable insights, what you think, how you feel, and what you do next.

WHAT DOES YOUR DEFAULT FUTURE LOOK LIKE?

What happens in the categories listed if nothing changes?

FAMILY:

....

....

HEALTH:

....

....

CAREER:

....

....

FRIENDSHIPS:

....

....

PERSONALLY:

....

....

FINANCE:

....

....

SPIRITUALLY/INSPIRATIONALLY:

....

....

OTHER:

....

....

BONUS

I decided to create some support for those who read the book and are ready to do the work. It is a private accountability pacesetter where you can get custom reminders about what you committed to doing and, most importantly, why. If you showed up ready to do the work and you want to check it out, I invite you to visit SuccessHangover.com and look for the Accountability link. That's where you will sign up to receive stepped and staged emails that will keep you on pace to set the goals, do the work, and enact the change you came for. Sometimes surviving one's own success can be as hard as creating it in the first place. I'd like to support you in making it easier.

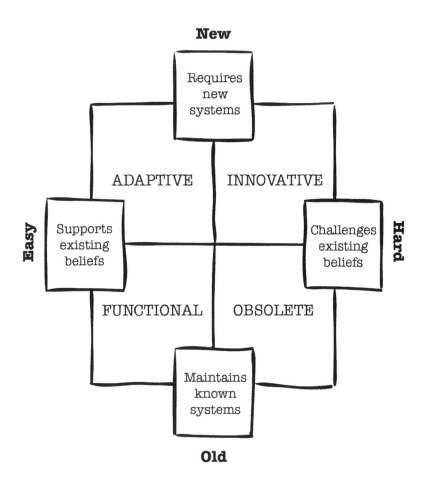

New

Requires new systems

ADAPTIVE   INNOVATIVE

Easy

Supports existing beliefs   Challenges existing beliefs

Hard

FUNCTIONAL   OBSOLETE

Maintains known systems

Old

QUADRANT EXERCISE

Sometimes we find ourselves stuck in a holding pattern, a status quo conundrum, and with a default future that looks little like the ideal future we imagined.

Approached with the usual question of "What do I want to do or change?" we rarely find concrete options or ways forward that illicit action. The question is too broad, too opaque, and spans far too many facets of our life and career that the rush of potential responses overlap. The answer is muddy, so we get overwhelmed. We have too many ideas, yet too little clarity in any tactical or strategic direction.

After I was diagnosed with cancer, I went into a state of overwhelm. I wanted to overhaul my status quo and create a new default future—one that would make me feel alive and in control again. I developed this model during that process.

When looking at my life, I have found that, not only after the cancer conundrum but also since, this model has served to help answer those questions by simplifying the analysis. How? By looking at areas of my life, habits, and environment such that I can see where I am feeding systems that no longer serve me, those that hold me back, or those that stretch me in unproductive ways.

If you complete this exercise with honesty, you should find areas ripe for change or adaptation—those where stasis is warranted.

- Where do I spend time in old patterns that no longer guide me in the direction I want to go?
- Where do I focus my energy on outdated actions, driving me into unintentional obsolescence?
- What areas should I revisit to determine if the system within which I operate reflects my current reality, capacity, or wants?
- Where am I stagnating and where am I stretching?
- What beliefs do I hold that I've not tested, and which of them may stagnate my growth?
- What quadrants are under- or overserved? What can I do to change this now?

HOW TO COMPLETE THIS EXERCISE

STEP 1

You can hand draft this little model or visit the website and print off a shiny new copy for your self-assessment and growth pleasure: SuccessHangover.com.

STEP 2

On a blank piece of paper, write down all the things you spend your time or energy doing. This list can be as exhaustive as you like and can focus on career/business or life alone, or a combination of both. Simply write until you feel you have run out of things to capture. Write things you feel are positive, negative, and neutral. If you are like me, you may need up to three pages. If you are like some clients of mine, one page will do. Remember, no one is looking at the page(s), so be as honest as you can.

Next, focus on a few of the highest resonating things— those with the greatest emotional charge—and ask yourself why. Why do I do this? What belief or value do I hold that is connected to the reason for this action, pattern, and trait? You can jot that down on the scrap paper, as it will help you in the next step. If the question "Why?" did not help for some, ask yourself "How?" What system are you using or operating within that supports you in consistently taking this action? Jot that down.

If you want to go ninja level, simply open the floodgates and see what has been left unsaid. To do this, I ask myself, "And what else?"

EXAMPLE

Responding to incessant emails constantly.

Why? I suppose because I feel that responsive people seem to have their shit together more than people who sit on emails or don't reply when I need an answer right away. And because I long for the feeling of "complete" or "in control" and when emails are unread or unanswered, I feel like I'm failing. My actions support the belief that responding to emails on demand is more important than holding to my own plans and priorities.

How? I work with my laptop almost all day. I have alerts that come across my screen when emails come in. My cell is always near. I see that damn red dot, and the growing number of new emails is a constant reminder. I use technology to systematically alert me to new and unanswered emails.

But here's the thing: when I'm the most responsive person on the block, it only creates more emails. Essentially, I'm training people to ask me (because I answer) rather than figure shit out for themselves. I feel a sense of sick pride when I am the first to reply to emails on a thread when sent to a group, that it helps me influence group outcomes when I set a tone for my position first. I feel slighted or unimportant when people do not reply to my emails right away, and there is something in me that does not want any of my friends, family, or business partners to feel that I do not care for them—and I show them that by being responsive. But I am assuming that my emailing them back right away is received as care when really, who knows if they even care how fast I reply? Truth be told, I also like to have a written record of some things, because I find that people like to remember whatever they like from discussions. Emails help me keep an account of important things.

STEP 3

Plot each item within one of the four quadrants.

- **Innovative.** Challenges your existing beliefs and requires you to adopt new systems.
- **Obsolete.** Challenges your existing beliefs and allows you to maintain a known system to serve it.
- **Functional.** Supports your existing beliefs, and you use a known system to maintain it.
- **Adaptive.** Supports your existing beliefs but requires you to adopt a new system to support it.

To utilize the example above, I would plot responding to emails in the Obsolete quadrant, because the way I feel about it challenges my beliefs insofar as it begs me to ask myself if I truly believe the thoughts and emotions connected to doing this task, and how I continue to complete the task maintains my existing system of notifications and automatically responding to them.

STEP 4

Observe what you have plotted and ask yourself, "Where can I make changes to serve me?"

STEP 5

Make changes.

On a blank, new diagram of the model, map out where things would sit if you made changes.

For example, I would replot my email scenario to Adaptive as I align myself with the beliefs I truly have about emails—when I'm showing up as my best self, free of judgment and self-sabotage. I would be utilizing new systems of putting my phone in airplane mode when working or during family time, and shutting down the mail program while doing work that requires me to focus and maintain a period of flow.

STEP 6

Compare the two models (new and old). How do you feel about them?

Take a few minutes to jot down what you observe and feel. If you are keen to maintain ninja mode, future cast what life will be like when you live up to your own expectations within the new model of living.

BONUS STEP

Reach out: shoot me an email or tag me on the socials with what you have done, how you feel, and with your questions. Connect with me, and let's embed a little bit of social proof, a declaration of your commitment to show up in a new way.

@kelseyramsden

Kelsey@SuccessHangover.com

I can't wait to hear from you.

What I do NOT WANT:

_____

_____

_____

_____

_____

_____

_____

_____

_____

WHAT I DO *NOT* WANT

So often, it is easier to state what we do not want, the things that irk us, drag us down, hold us back. Somehow, when we are at the very, very early stages of the next growth period, we feel quite badly. It's often this discomfort that compels us to disrupt our stasis and screw the status quo—but toward what purpose?

Let's face it, if you made it this far in this book, you are a rebel of some sort. You are likely the kind of person who does not sit on the sidelines long when change needs to be made. But now that you have something to lose, we want to be sure that upsetting the apple cart leaves some apples with which to still make pie.

I'm an optimist and a big fan of good vibes, but let's face it, sometimes we have to wade through some shit to get to greener pastures. So let's do it.

In completing this exercise, we will assess our constructive discomfort and focus our attention squarely on shifting from being stuck in the mud to allowing the mud to provide nutrients to our locus. In simple terms, we will flip the bad to the good and create some clarity and strategy to carry you through upsetting the apple cart purposefully.

STEP 1

Mosey on over to the site to print off the latest and greatest template to complete the exercise below. Trust me, blank pages allow folks like us to veer off, whereas set pages are like targets where we can laser focus our minds in record time: SuccessHangover.com.

STEP 2

Create an exhaustive list of what you do not want—that is, things, people, and situations that no longer serve you in showing up and creating the next act, your best life in this next era.

Go on, let the page have it.

STEP 3

For each item you listed, imagine that they spontaneously vanished. How would you feel? List the emotion.

STEP 4

Take responsibility; assign control. For each item, think about your responsibility for it and whether or not you have control or influence over it. On a scale from one to ten, with one being no control whatsoever and ten being full control, assign each item a number.

STEP 5

Although it is popular at the present time to go around talking about creating space and expanding, I think this guidance is a heap of baloney. There are no voids created. Empty space is filled. It's that simple. So while we may create space for a near infinitesimal period, it will soon become filled with something else, someone else, drama, a project, our thoughts, something—anything. For people like us, there is no vacancy.

Start with the items you marked as ten and ask yourself, "If not this, then what?"

Move on to the items marked nine and so on until you arrive to those marked five. Now ask yourself, do you really want to spend your time bearing responsibility for the things you can't impact? Too harsh?

STEP 6

Once you have answered, "If not this, then what?" for each response, consider asking yourself how the thing you chose to fill the void will serve you, specifically in supporting your next success, defying your status quo, and igniting you to feel alive again. To be blunt, why bother? Are you running away from something or toward something? If it is toward, you have a winner. If it is simply away, try again and focus your attention through the windshield, not the rearview mirror. What can you fill the void with that compels you to stay fixed on the future?

STEP 7

Get the feels.

Spoiler alert: later in the book, you will find out what embeds knowledge, and although I can't footnote a study, we know what maintains actions to be the same thing— feelings. If it feels good, we do more of it. So let's prime the feel-good motor. For each item you have flipped and filled with an adapted focus, drop in one or two words on how it will make you feel.

STEP 8

Commit to that shift. Lists are great, but they are just

lists. It's like how having a hammer does not make you a carpenter.

I know if you went to the great effort to really do this exercise all the way, you are not a half-asser. You know by now that I'm not either. Let's do this thing together. Send me a pic of your list or shoot me an email with your top one or two actions. What did you find? What will you fill the void with, by when, and what for? How does it make you feel?

HIT ME UP ON EMAIL OR TAG ME IN A POST ABOUT IT

Kelsey@SuccessHangover.com

@kelseyramsden

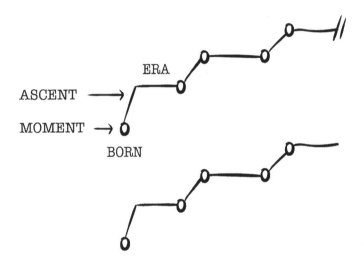

ASCENT ⟶

ERA

MOMENT →

BORN

What have been your top of mountain moments, your eras, turning points, your ascents?

STEP FUNCTION MODEL

This is a quick and easy exercise that allows you to track your past and future pace, while being realistic about the time it takes to gather the necessary ingredients (people, experience, knowledge, wisdom) during plateau periods to fuel up for another ascent.

You can scoop blank copies of this model at the website or deface this one, whichever your fancy.

STEP 1

Circles denote the beginning of an ascent or a milestone. Plateaus denote the time you spent between ascents. The goal here is to look at how far you have come, where you want to go, and to allow yourself to see that some plateaus are required, some belabored, and some can be abbreviated if we approach them as such.

Fill in the circles of your past.

Denote things during the plateaus you now see are required in order to reach the next circle. Do the same during the periods of ascent. These can be courses, people, and experiences. Just jot down the essential ingredients *you* need to reach that next plotted point on the step function graph.

STEP 2

Now what? Looking ahead, what will denote the beginning of an ascent? Where are you headed (milestone), and what will you need during that plateau to either catch your breath from the last blast upward or to prepare for the next one? How long does it need to be? How long do you want it to be? How will you know when it is time to engage?

Plot the points and make notes along the lines that join them.

STEP 3

Do something about it. Taking action in the moment is key to bringing ideas from the page into life.

- What can you do right now?

- Will you do it?

I sure as heck hope you do something. After all, isn't it in our nature to make things happen?

INGREDIENTS ON YOUR MENTAL SHELF.

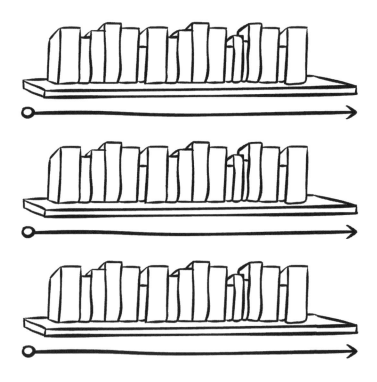

INGREDIENTS ON YOUR MENTAL SHELF

What are you working with? It's easy to knowledge-drop degrees and major life experiences, but often it's in the nuance of experience, connections, emotions, and values that we find the exponential effect of our unique ability.

STEP 1

On the bottom two shelves, write on the spine of each book things you know, knowledge assets you have stored on your mental shelves. It's OK if they are somewhat general. Examples: MBA, Cash Flow Analysis, BEcon.

STEP 2

On the second shelf, write on the spine of each book

things that you remember. Memories that resonate emotionally and bubble up first will do, just whatever you remember.

STEP 3

On the top shelf, write on the spine of each book either knowledge or memories with an emotional charge that you have stocked in the past three months.

STEP 4

Gut-check and assess.

Look at all you have stocked on your shelves. Is there anything missing? Anything underutilized? Anything you might take off the shelf and throw in the waste bin?

There is a way of looking at this; it's called skill stacking. It involves looking at the things you have stocked that can be combined in a new way, a way you've not used them before, or simply a way that is unique to you. This is where the gold is. How can you mine it today or over the next while?

Let me know. I'm curious as to what you have stocked and what you find. If you want to head over to the website, you can see my shelves and the way I draw lines between the books to create new connections, ways to see what I have collected on my shelves, and the strategy I use to fill the top shelf with only the best volumes. I'll have notes on what I do next, which might help you draw your own lines and next steps.

See you there: www.SuccessHangover.com.

INTRODUCE YOURSELF.

I am: Kelsey Ramsden.

I am a: A creator.

Who deeply values: Intimate connection.

___

I am: ___

I am a: ___

Who deeply values: ___

INTRODUCE YOURSELF

Simple yet deeply effective—almost lightning-bolt stuff—this exercise will help you shed labels and drive at the through line of what keeps you engaged, what shows up in everything you truly love and desire, and what will bring you to your next act.

STEP 1

Without stating any of the following:

- Where you are from
- Where you live
- What education you have
- What you do for employment
- Hobbies you have for enjoyment
- How many children you have bred or animals you have

- How many siblings you have
- What you study
- Your relationship status
- Your gender

NOW TRY TO INTRODUCE YOURSELF

Who are you? What underlies all the items above that you might have traditionally listed within your intro? Parse out what's driven you as a core emotion or interest throughout most of the things you would want to be known for, through how you choose to introduce yourself. After all, an introduction is our opportunity to frame, up front, how we want others to see us.

EXAMPLE

A traditional intro might look like this:

I am Kelsey Ramsden, award-winning businesswoman, cancer survivor, and mother of three. I am from a small town in Canada called Kelowna but now live with my husband, children, and two dogs in London, Ontario. When I am not running my businesses in construction and real estate, I travel the world speaking to groups about innovation and entrepreneurship—that I'm an underdog makes for a good story. In my spare time, I love to plan parties, host dinners, and go to live music shows. I have an MBA but believe that experience is greater than knowledge.

ANALYSIS

When I meet people, I use titles, awards, status, and accomplishments. Ultimately, I use buckets that help a person understand me, by categorizing myself in ways they can understand. These are broad and common buckets that feel safe and show the best of me in what I have done, not necessarily who I am.

Do I introduce myself this way because I want someone to know and understand me, or because it's safe? If I'm honest, I introduce myself this way because it lends to easy surface-level conversations, and positions me as accomplished and important. *Eeww*, that even felt sick to write. Sometimes the truth hurts.

NEXT LEVEL

Few accomplished and driven people are satisfied with surface-level interactions. Let's face it, we have only so much time and likely already have all of the friends we need. What we are looking for is something much more engaging. We want to know where the true action is, and we want our conversations to look like this, too. We're beyond getting to know your résumé; we want to take it to the next level.

GETTING DOWN TO IT

For me, I came to recognize that no matter what age I was or where I was in my career and life, what garnered true attention and devotion (where I kicked ass and delivered results that even surprised me) resulted from the times when I was creating something. Creating life, ideas, businesses, friendships, moments, a home, connecting ideas, and discussing through talks, books, podcasts—all of it involved creating. I could not help it. Everywhere I went and in everything I excelled at, I found a way to create. For me, it was always about creating. And when I could not create, I stagnated—dead on the inside, held back, frustrated, even caged.

So what?

Why do I feel the need to create? What is it about that thing I source in every aspect of my life and career that drives me to never want to stop doing it? What about it—the process, the feeling, the work, the joy and pain—keeps me coming back? Creating for the sake of it is not enough. I know this. We all know that there is a deeper why to the things we do.

If you are finding it challenging to respond to this, you

might consider asking yourself why about five times. You do this by asking "Why?," responding, then asking "Why?" to that response, and repeating this five more times. It's a guaranteed way to quickly get in the deep. I find my responses generally get uncomfortable around the third why.

When I'm at my best—I'm talking about the times when I'm in the flow and happy to show up with my fullest potential, warts and all—those are the times I'm intimately connected to the work or the people. It's the moment when there's a breakthrough, an undeniable shift in closeness and connection—when there is intimacy. It's a naked mind, fully charged, that is at the root of my thirst for life; it's what I live for. Those moments. It is my life's drug.

I am Kelsey Ramsden. I am a creator who deeply values intimate connection.

BRINGING IT BACK

Now read my original intro; can you see the threads? Can you see how my shorter, deeper intro tells you so much more about who I am versus what I choose to do?

Of course, there are times when each introduction would yield an appropriate conversation to follow based on the person and place, but can you see how this introduction can be useful as a reintroduction to self?

How do you think you can use this to decipher opportunities from distractions, ways forward when you're stuck, as you approach your next act? How do you think you can utilize this to identify things that can make you feel alive again?

I can't wait to meet you; I'd love for you to introduce yourself to me.

Send me an email with your newly crafted intro: Kelsey@SuccessHangover.com.

Until then...

WHAT ARE YOU FEEDING YOUR MIND?

I like to tackle this one with a strong coffee and some great music in the background; it's a free-form kind of thing that works best when you don't overthink it.

The goal is to look at what we feed our minds. Simple, really.

If we can agree that the human mind is wired to consume information, wired to learn, then this exercise allows us to look at what we are feeding the machine. If inputs equal outputs, then it can provide a great snapshot and allow one to discern what kind of output can be expected from the current inputs. Better yet, we can look at holes in the inputs that can be filled to give us the kind of output we really want for a fully charged mind.

STEP 1

Again, this is a free-form kind of exercise, so you can prompt the flow of responses by prodding yourself by asking a few different things. I will give you some ideas on ways to prod your gray matter below.

Once the ideas start to flow, simply jot them down around the picture of the brain. You don't need to worry about categories or quadrants. Just write.

A few ways you could get started:

- Think of all the things over the past week that have passed through your senses and left a footprint on your mind.
- Think of a usual day; what habits or patterns do you have that feed your mind?
- Whom do you spend time with? What info or stimuli does spending time with them feed your mind?
- Where do you get information, new or old, and what kind of information does it serve your brain?
- Where do you physically spend your time (traveling, standing, sitting, working, socializing, etc.), and what kind of information does that serve?
- What inner thoughts do you parade around daily, and what do you say to yourself?

STEP 2

Once you have filled the page, and you should be able to (you are feeding your mind something every waking minute of the day either consciously or subconsciously), have a look at what you see.

I like to imagine feeding my brain much like how we give our bodies nutrition. There are some things that are essential to our very survival, some things that are nutritionally packed; some things that might be delicious but not at all nutritious; and some things I consume that are straight-up junk food or even hurt me.

When you look at all the things surrounding your brain on that page, consider getting some colored pencils or pens and circle the things you consider essential, things you consider nutritional, and the junk food—the harmful stuff. Identify where your mental diet might be lacking.

STEP 3

This step isn't necessary, but if you are keen and like to go the distance with things, I recommend that you do a second draft—a mind menu of sorts that takes only the best things you are already feeding your mind, and that includes the things you want to start feeding your mind.

You can download a fresh brain page over at the site if you want to do it right: SuccessHangover.com.

Some people create vision boards with scraps of paper from magazines, complete with cutout cars and watches, or pictures of skinny people on beaches. That's cool. I do one every New Year's Day; it's a fun art/visualization project, but I never find it gives me nearly the depth of insight or huge value strategically and tactically that doing this exercise does.

When I'm feeling in a rut, doubtful, frustrated, stuck in stasis, or uninspired, I pull out my mind menu, and it's always obvious within a few seconds what I could be feeding my mental engine to supercharge it for best performance.

When I am on a roll and feeling great, I pull out the same piece of paper so I can see exactly where I am getting my high-octane fuel from—or even add new things to the map that I know deliver big returns for me mentally.

I don't know about you for certain, but I can say with 100 percent confidence that my mind is the engine that drives everything for me, and if I don't give the machine what it runs best on, the results are a foregone conclusion.

OPEN QUESTIONS FOR WITNESSING?

How do I feel psychologically, emotionally, mentally?

Questions:

_____   _____
_____   _____
_____   _____
_____   _____
_____   _____
_____   _____
_____   _____
_____   _____

QUESTIONS FOR WITNESSING

With all of your experience, knowledge, education, and intuition, it can be hard to suspend judgment and simply witness things. I'll never claim to be deeply knowledgeable about the concept of "presence" so many people talk about these days. I make my best attempt at being present in moments, ideas, and conversations, without jumping to and fro by quickly overlaying judgment (good, bad, or otherwise) and potentially missing opportunities or expanding blind spots because of it.

I remember someone once telling me that if everything around you is somehow negative, it might be that the common denominator is you. This really pissed me off, with the kind of pang that only truth delivers to the hearts of the "right." I took this comment to heart and looked at the challenging people, conversations, and business situations that surrounded me at the time. I decided to ask myself some questions to try and maintain a presence that allowed me to more fully see not only the situations I was in but also myself within them.

START WITH THE FIVE SENSES

After cancer, I asked my oncologist if it was possible to see color more brightly after surviving such an experience. He said it wasn't. I still think it is, but that is neither here nor there. Why this matters to us in this conversation is that this experience of a heightened sense was one of the first keys to the idea of witnessing for me—getting more into the five senses and out of my head so much.

What if I actually looked, listened, felt, smelled, and tasted things? What would I come to understand if I allowed these things to be experienced as opposed to assumed or presumed based on past judgment or experience?

To use a ridiculous example for simplicity, what about a bite of a hot dog? What is a hot dog like? Think about it. Do you even experience eating a hot dog anymore (or an apple for you veggie folks)?

We might think of it as either hot or cold. Are either bad or good? When was the last time you sensed something for observational purposes as opposed to immediate categorical purposes?

Do you think there is a way to be taken back to the first time? Can you witness a thing for what it is now, as who you are now? Suspend categorization. Experience first, question your experience, then allow yourself to impose judgment.

FOLLOW THE HEART

It's OK to feel and then to question what's behind those chemical rushes that can mislead us into judgment without a second thought. Are you truly afraid or simply experiencing fear? There is a nuance there that I will use an example to illustrate. You're in the shower, you reach for the hair conditioner, and in picking up the bottle, you reveal a spider. The spider is brown and black and big enough that you think you can make out his eyes, multiple of them.

It's likely you sense a rush of emotion as a result; perhaps you even respond by smashing the spider with the bottle of conditioner, or you eject yourself through the shower door at a speed not seen in ages. Whatever your response to the experience of emotion, I wonder, after you either kill that beast or run away, do you laugh at yourself?

What do you see through this experience that proves a

potential rush to judgment? Do you think that witnessing our emotions can provide useful data points? Can they demand we pay attention to the experience of the emotion and potentially disassociate the emotion from the stimuli? Is there value in looking at what we feel and allowing ourselves to have these emotions become feelings other than extrapolating a reality from them?

Do you think this presence of mind could be helpful in times of pressure or stress in business and relationships? What about joy and elation, even the sensation of love?

Do you think it's possible to witness an experience anew? Observe it as opposed to judging it based on your chemical experience?

A note of caution is worth mentioning here, and it relates to intuition. I firmly believe that intuition is the sum of all of our experience rolled into a sensation that is inexplicable in the same way that trying to explain how one walks is inexplicable: we just do. It's a know-how we picked up over the ages. It's impossible to put into words, it's complex, and we take it for granted. The caution here is that I would never want one to ignore intuition. If you sense someone is watching you, they probably are. If you sense you should not hire someone, you probably should not. I think we can all agree that the sensation of intuition is very different than an emotion. Intuition is a sensation of knowing, not feeling. I think it's important to make this clear because intuition can be a powerful indicator; it can still be witnessed, but it should be done so with caution, as it's more difficult to find the signal in the noise.

FINISH WITH THE MIND

Damn, you're clever. This can be one of your greatest problems. When you have big mental horsepower, it can be easy to judge quickly because you simply know so much—sometimes too much.

I think the best way to approach witnessing of our own thoughts is to start with a differentiation between choices and decisions. Decisions are made often because the way forward seems almost a given, it's obvious to us. Because of the mass of our knowledge, we can take for granted and not even observe when we decide things without seeing and weighing choice: the opportunity to weigh and assess different alternatives equally.

Our great horsepower causes us to move quickly. The first step is to rein in those horses. *Whoa!* Slow down the decisions and look for choice.

A simple example that occurs daily for most of us is in our way to work or school. I wonder, which way you go? Is it the same every time? Likely it is. Why? Is it faster, more straightforward, known? I wonder, are there alternate routes? Do they have merit? Are they prettier, more interesting, do they take you past a new coffee stop? Many of us select the most direct route when another route that is more enjoyable might take five minutes more. Could waking up five minutes earlier yield a better start to your day? Decisions versus choice: every day, more often than we think.

A more advanced exercise is available to us when we look at meetings. An item is on the table for discussion, and before anyone speaks, we often have made our decision, we have a conclusion, and we have a way forward. We judge all future statements or offerings of insight provided on the subject based on our finish point. We skip the middle, we miss the choice, and we omit witnessing in favor of certainty and safety through starting with the decision and weighing all things to it.

WITNESS

For yourself, right now, look around or select a recent occurrence and jot down notes about how you might have witnessed it differently had you been thinking in the terms above. What might have occurred to you? How would the experience have been different? Could there have been opportunities you missed? What benefit could you have gained using the witnessing principle to be more present?

Are there questions you can ask yourself to bring your attention back to witnessing when you begin to slip into racehorse mode with that grand mind of yours, and your life's experience charging you forward, potentially missing things in the now? Can you think of prompts that may drive you back to choice making, as opposed to being in the autopilot of decision making?

Mark where you fall on the spectrum by drawing an X on the line.

COURAGE ├────────────┤ COMFORT

Health ├────────────┤

Family ├────────────┤

Friends ├────────────┤

Work ├────────────┤

Knowledge ├────────────┤

──────── ├────────────┤

──────── ├────────────┤

──────── ├────────────┤

COURAGE AND COMFORT

A few years back, I was invited to an exclusive gathering of entrepreneurs in Austin, Texas. The host brought in a woman whom I had not heard of before; her name was Brené Brown. Since then, her popularity has skyrocketed, and she's written numerous best sellers involving her research on courage, vulnerability, shame, and empathy. She is a downright dynamo, and I highly recommend any and all her work—period.

At this particular event, she was speaking about the distance between courage and comfort and that you cannot have both at the same time. Her comment and deep research on the subject hit me like a lightning storm or a flurry of left hooks. What a clear and eloquent way to discern where I am hiding out, where I might be bravely taking action, and where I might be in a place that feels right for the moment.

I must give credit where it is due: after Brené Brown's talk, I left the day's sessions and returned to my hotel room. There, I began to draw lines on a page to assess where I sat on the spectrum of courage and comfort within many areas of my life. I followed each X with an O (to note where I would like to be). Then I listed three things I could do to move closer to the O for each. It took me three tries to be honest with myself about where the X and O ought to fall, but I got there.

Building from that day some five years ago, I decided to take a page out of my own book and expand on the practice, demanding myself to explore how it would feel to live closer to the O: how I expected to feel when I got there and what I would get out of it.

As I've said in this book, there will be some level of constructive discomfort, and I wanted to be able to predict it in those cases where I was moving toward courage. Conversely, comfort is a feeling I've fled from all my life. I think it's based on a core belief I somehow embedded, that the things worth achieving should be hard, and if things were easy, I was either slacking or oblivious to pending threat. I no longer believe this, but the fear of comfort, of stillness, of being satisfied is a reality for me, so I wanted to be able to shine light on what I know to be my own instinctual response to sufficiency. Alas, I added the "How I will feel," "How I will know," and "How it serves me."

It's a pretty straightforward exercise meant to help you see some of the same things we have been exploring through a different lens. Much like glasses, we rarely know if our prescription is slightly off until we try a few different lenses to confirm how we see a thing is indeed closer to or further from 20/20.

You can get extra copies of this exercise at the website: SuccessHangover.com.

This one is a book club favorite. If your book club is anything like mine (and includes a few glasses of wine), then when everyone brings this exercise completed to the discussion, you'll have a night of big shifts, deep connection, perhaps even some tears—but guaranteed a lot of laughs.

COMPETENCE
(TACTICAL)

CONFIDENCE
(EMOTIONAL)

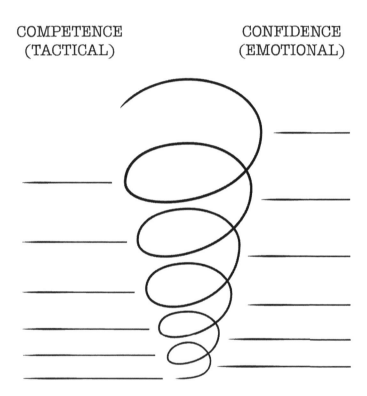

CONFIDENCE AND COMPETENCE

To me, confidence and competence are like the career and life, chicken and egg. You know, the old question about which came first?

When we were young, we tried things. No one learned to ride their bike the first time they got on. Yet as we age, we elevate our expectations for performance almost as if our high-water mark permeates all aspects of our lives. If we are decent at a thing, we want to be decent at all things. If we're honest with ourselves, we expect greatness. But how can we expect greatness when, to continue to elevate and grow, we must learn? Learning requires unknowing either via knowledge acquisition or experience. To go from where you are to where you want to go next, which must come first: confidence or competence?

- **Competence**: the ability to do something successfully or efficiently.
- **Confidence**: a feeling of self-assurance arising from one's appreciation of one's own abilities or qualities.

When I deliver talks, I often hand out postcards to the audience and ask them, much like the courage and confidence exercise we just completed pages before, to map out where on the spectrum they are operating in various areas of their lives. If we are looking at career, are you operating from a place of solid competence, or are you stretching and require confidence to do so in order to develop greater competencies?

→ Enter blind confidence.

What about when you don't know what you don't know?

→ Enter competence bias.

What about when you believe you are better or worse than you might be judged by a panel of your peers?

Where competence can be tactical, confidence can be emotional, and both can be useful or detrimental depending on the pursuit.

How can we use this dance between confidence and competence to propel us forward? The only way I've found to help me see where I'm going is to look where I've been and to utilize my own track record as a forecast. Think of it like a great tornado of ascent, swirling back and forth with its great force propelling you upward—confidence and competence in a dance, encircling each other and propelling you through growth.

Take a look back and list those times you relied heavily on competence for the momentum you held. Alternately, when did you have to settle into appreciation of your own abilities and harness self-assurance? Or to push yourself through growth by utilizing confidence? Starting with your oldest touch points nearest the ground in the picture, go left to right, up the spiral: competence, confidence—development of a new competence and practicing it—then again needing confidence to step up, and back and forth you go until you reach today. So what's next?

The most important thing from here is to recognize where you are operating. Most often, are you in competence or confidence? What competencies do you want to develop and what self-assurance do you need to muster a move up the swirling ladder?

It can be dizzying, albeit comforting, once you start to predict the path.

I'd love to hear what you have decided your next elevated move is: diving into competence or stepping out to confidence. Take a picture and email it to me if you would. I'm so very curious about how our paths evolve and how our learning can bring us back to the same point at new levels. It's a subject I often find myself discussing with my closest friends and colleagues. I'd love to have that conversation with you, too. Shoot me a pic of what you find (penmanship not necessary) to Kelsey@SuccessHangover.com. I'll look forward to it.

RIP THIS PAGE OUT.

List activities, responsibilities,
relationships and anything else.

RIP AND RANK

Before those of you who like to keep books intact freak out, don't panic: you can download this page from the book site, and all will remain well in the world.

For those of you who are feeling a bit rebellious, get ready to tear a page out of a book.

I'm not sure about you, but many of my colleagues and friends talk about reaching periods of overwhelm. I feel overwhelm at its greatest when I'm approaching a pinnacle and I don't want to face the emptiness of the uncertainty that follows a big win or accomplishment—when I sense a change in the wind and suspect that my sights want to be reset. For me, "busy and responsible" is a great place to hide, until it's not.

For everyone, this exercise will approach different

opportunities or obstacles. For me, it culls the bullshit I let distract me; it reminds me where I have control and can focus the greatest of my attention and affection. For you, it might be something entirely different. What I can promise is that it will create a rank and file in your life that can't help but allow you to see old things anew and to focus or let go of some, too. It always helps to apportion energy and attention and create clear lines of responsibility for those things we can and cannot control. It can also be a slap in the face. How illuminating it can be to realize we're pacing toward a default future we don't want—and how quickly said future is approaching if we don't change anything.

STEP 1

Write all of the things that occupy your mind and time into these boxes, one per box. You can print more pages off at SuccessHangover.com. Alternately, if you are just dipping your toe in, you can jot down just the most relevant and important things that come to mind.

STEP 2

Circle those things you have 100 percent control over.

STEP 3

Rip or cut the page down and across the lines, creating little boxes, each with something you wrote in it, which you are now free to sort and stack.

Create your first stack from only the items you have circled.

STEP 4

Using all the items you did not circle, rank them in order of responsibility: from those you are most responsible for to those you are least responsible for. Have a look at them now, and don't read ahead. (Willpower will serve you well here.)

Take a moment to consider which you might move had I instructed you to rank them in order of importance or meaning. What about relevance to your long-term plans?

This is where I'd invite you to get curious: how can you rank these to see which things you carry in your mind and which occupy your time in new and different ways from different vantage points?

STEP 5

Journal: what did you find?

STEP 6

Take that pile of things you have 100 percent control of and imagine this:

You have hired someone to be the CEO of your life. They are in charge of making sure it goes the way you want it. All rights, responsibilities, and expectations are bestowed on them. (You already know where this is going, don't you?)

Now, tell me, if that staffer, that CEO, were coming up for review regarding items he or she is 100 percent in control of, what would you say to him or her?

Like all annual reviews, we should start with a positive and follow with an opportunity to improve.

Write yourself a review. Keep it. You might need it three months from now if you want to enroll in the private accountability pacesetter that I decided to create to support those who read the book and are ready to do the work. If that's you, I invite you to check out SuccessHangover. com and look for the Accountability link. That's where you will sign up to get stepped and staged emails that will keep you on pace to set the goals, do the work, and enact the change you came here for. You and I both know that sometimes surviving one's own success can be as hard as creating it in the first place. I'd like to support you in making it easier.

FIND THE OTHERS

This is a direct steal from Seth Godin in his book *What to Do When It's Your Turn*...and when you witness brilliance, sometimes there is no need to improve on it. Well, I did make a few slight changes, but basically, I stole this from Seth.

*Books don't change people. People change people.

We do it by sharing ideas, by setting standards, by making it clear that people like us do things like this. As Timothy Leary said, once you figure things out, it is your job to find the others.

Please share this copy with your team and with people you care about. You can get more copies by visiting SuccessHangover.com.

FIND THE OTHERS

Who should read this next? Write your name and then the names of the others. Pass this copy to them or get more, and do that thing that people like us do—give ideas.

....

....

....

....

....

....

The light at the end of the tunnel may be you.

—AEROSMITH, "AMAZING"

ABOUT THE AUTHOR

KELSEY RAMSDEN is an award-winning business mogul, author, entrepreneur and industry disruptor. She's ranked amongst the top women entrepreneurs in the world. She speaks around the globe at the likes of The Global Entrepreneurship Congress & The London School of Economics in addition to countless corporate events. She received her MBA from the University of Western Ontario and serves as a mentor for the Richard Branson Centre for Entrepreneurship.

Kelsey lives in Southwestern Ontario with her husband and three children. You can visit her at www.success hangover.com and follow her on Twitter and Instagram @kelseyramsden.

Printed in Great Britain
by Amazon